This book belongs to:

....

....

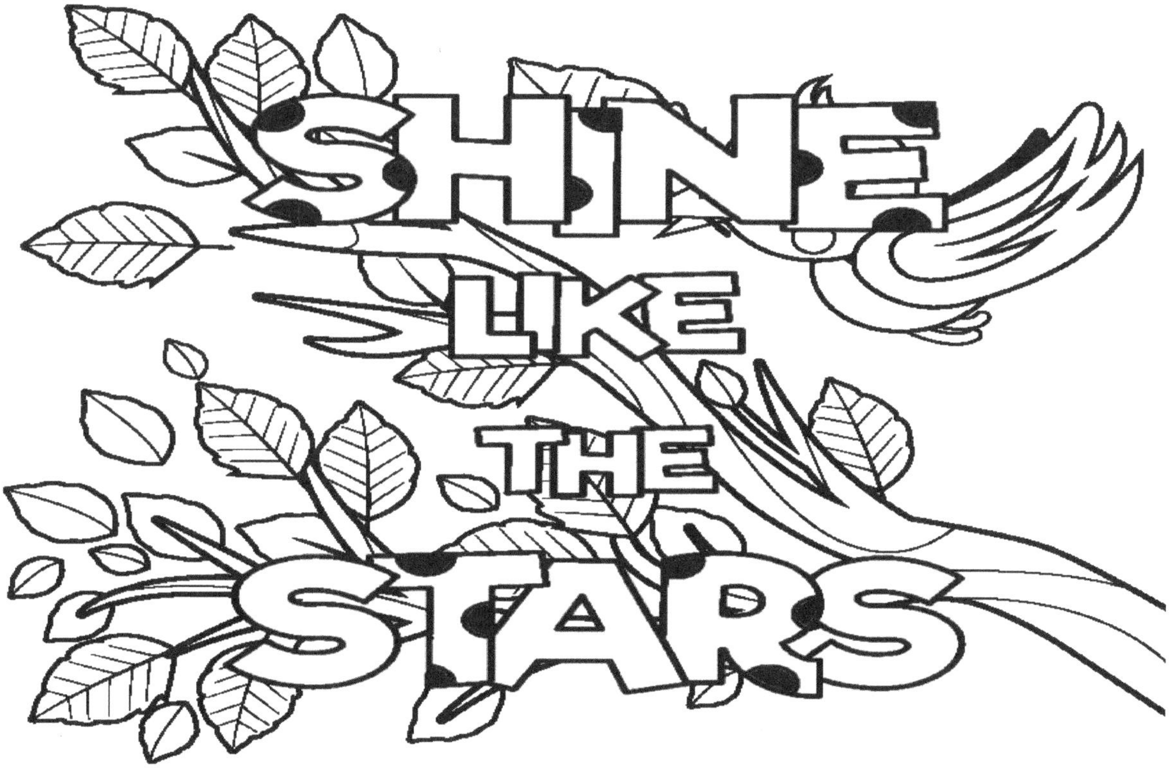

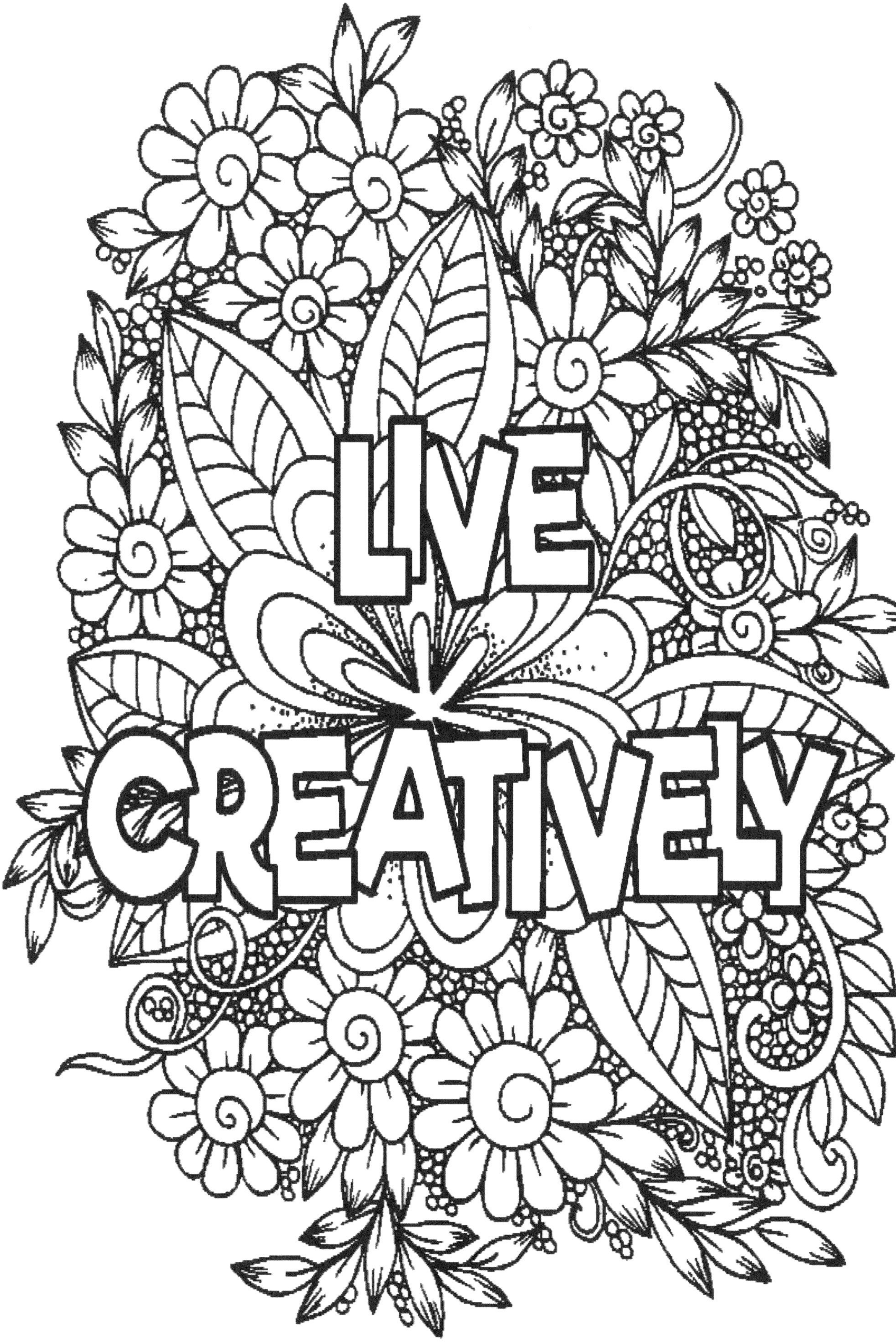
LIVE
CREATIVELY

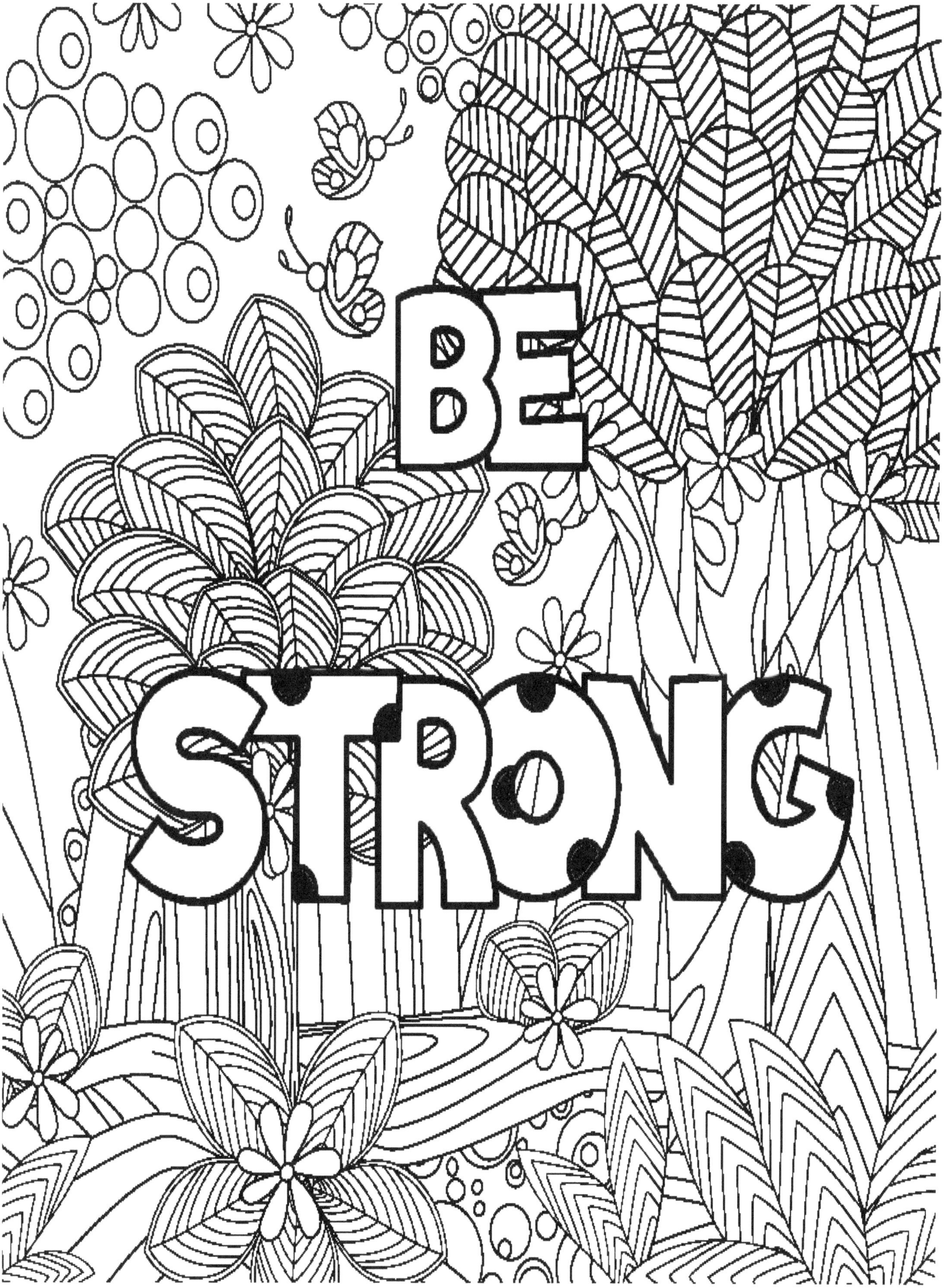
BE
STRONG

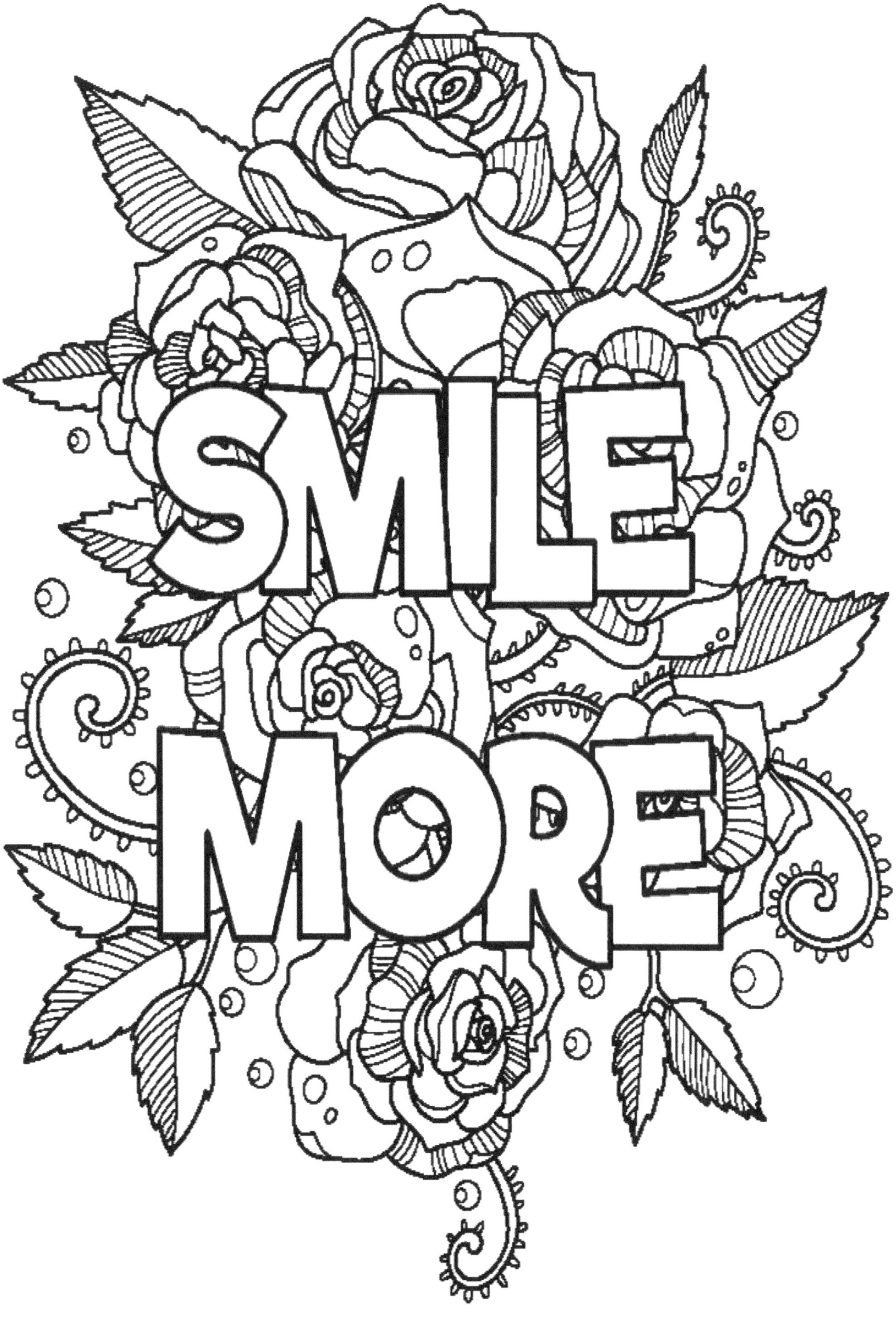
SMILE
MORE

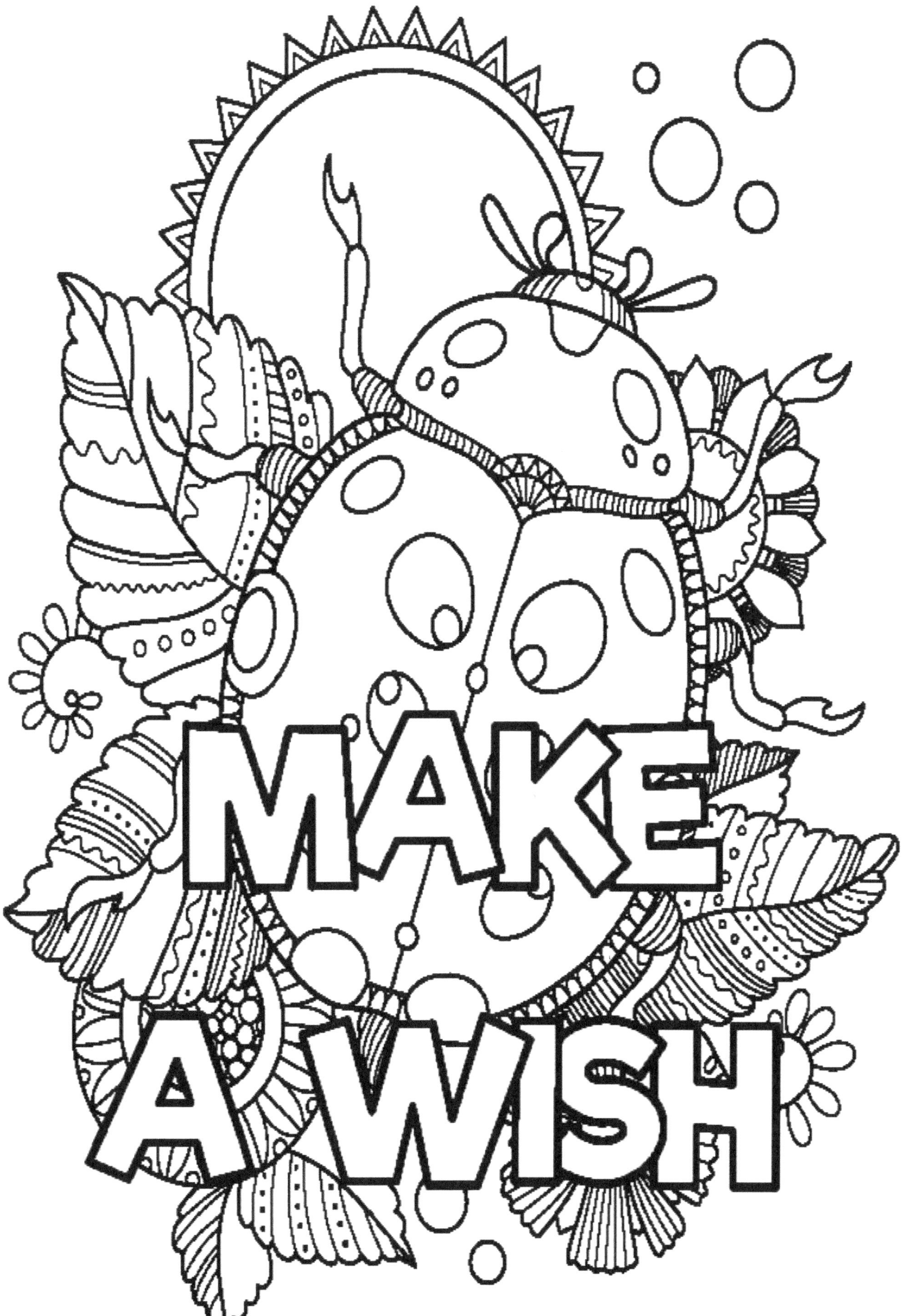
MAKE
A WISH

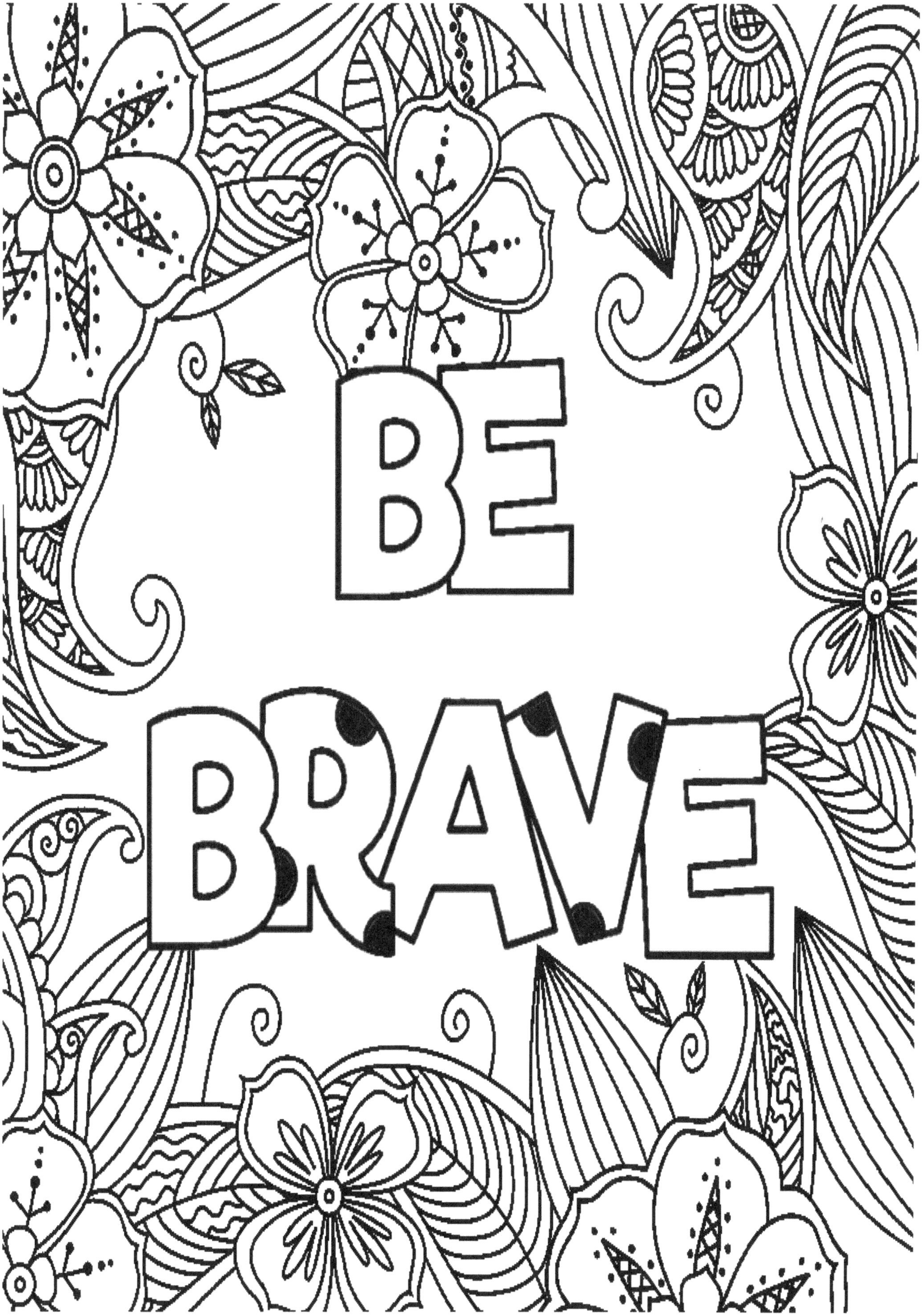
BE
BRAVE

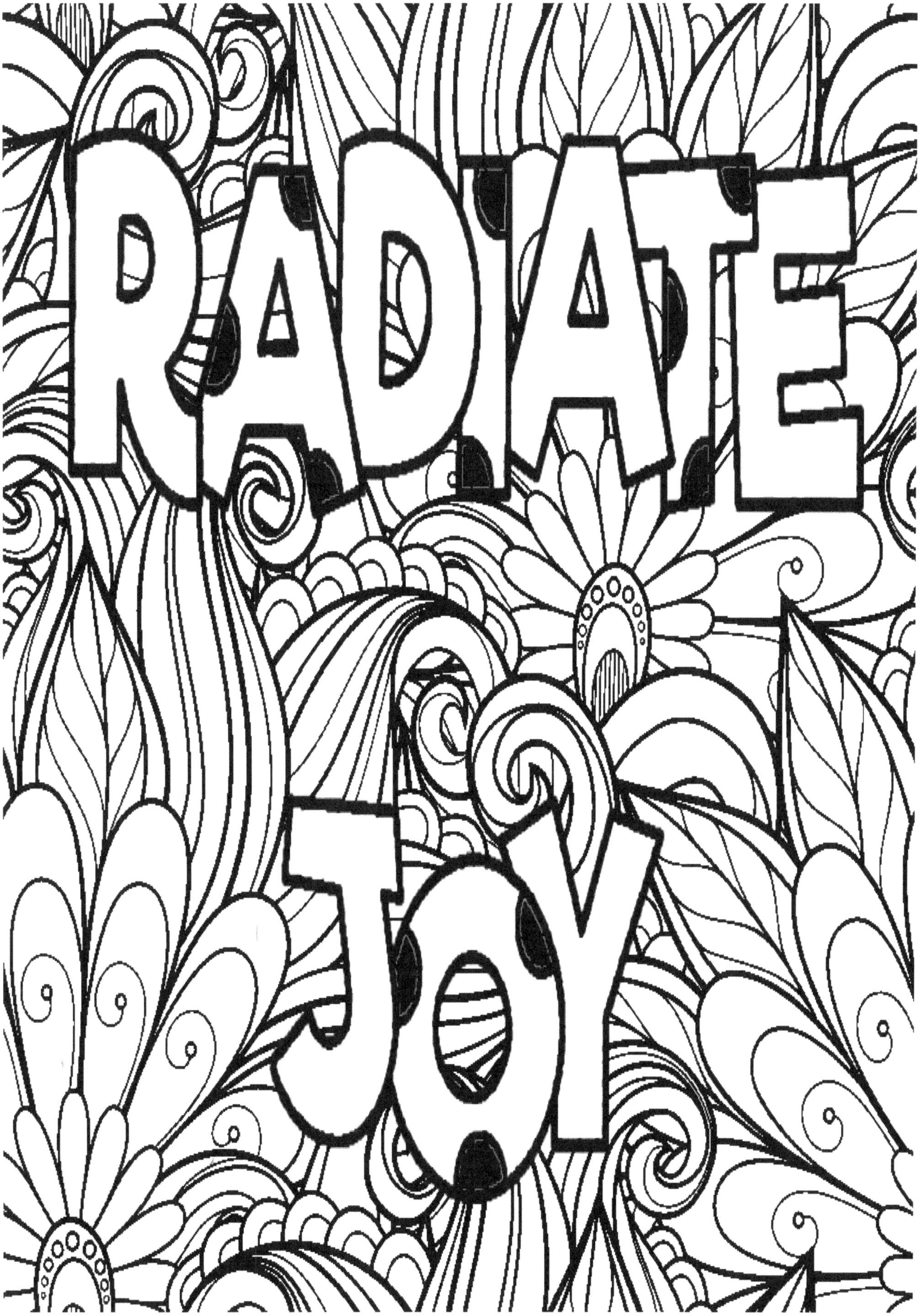
RADIATE
JOY

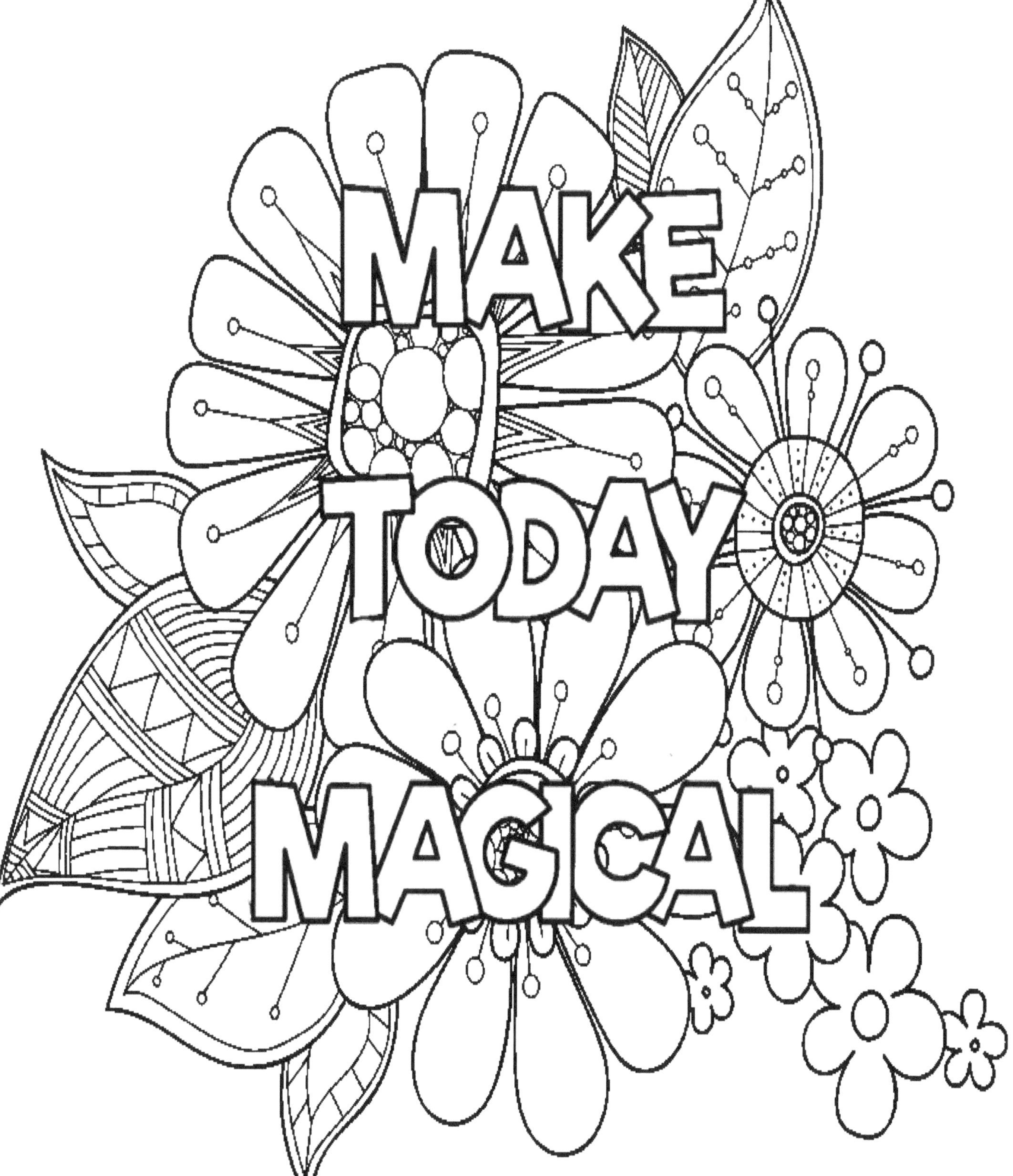
MAKE
TODAY
MAGICAL

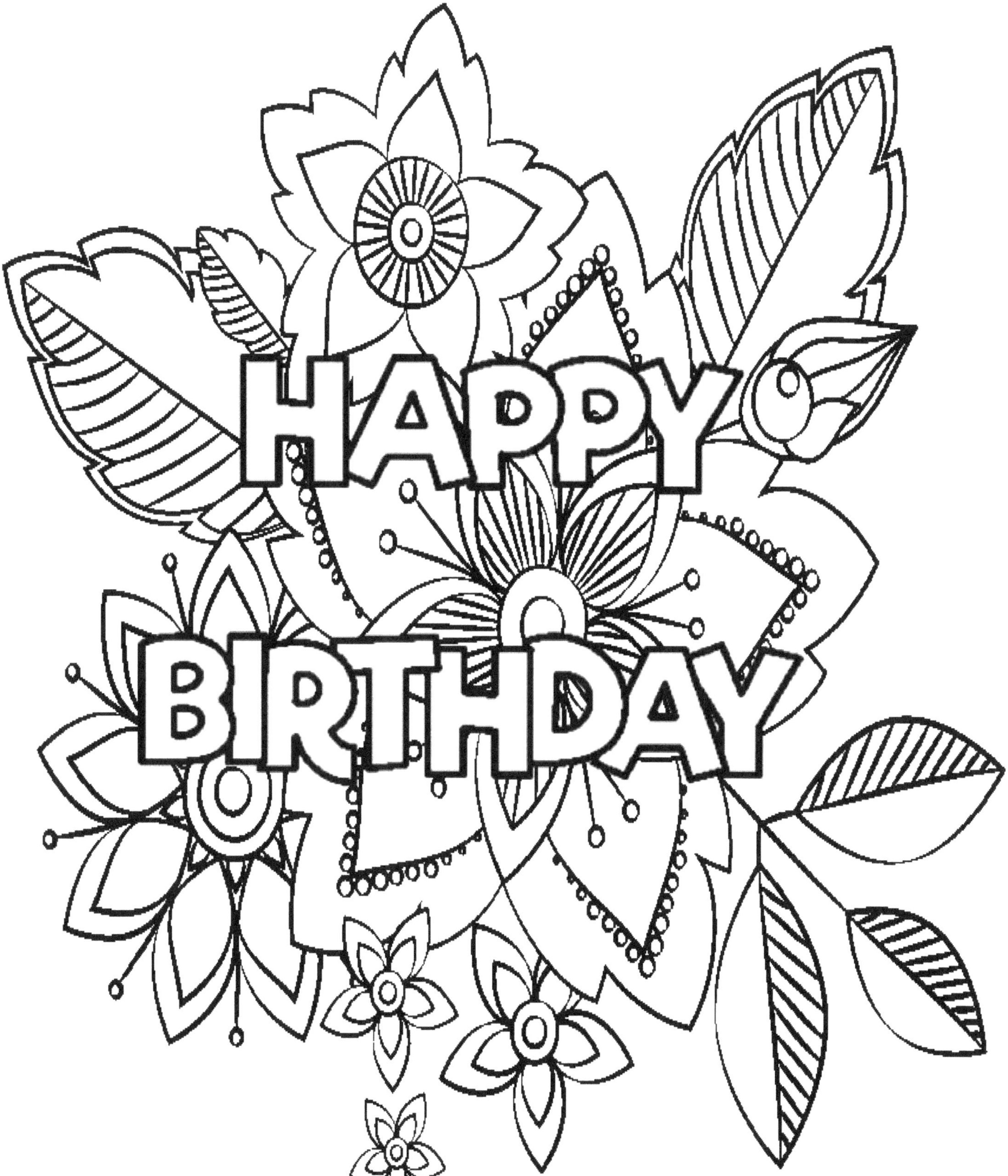
HAPPY
BIRTHDAY

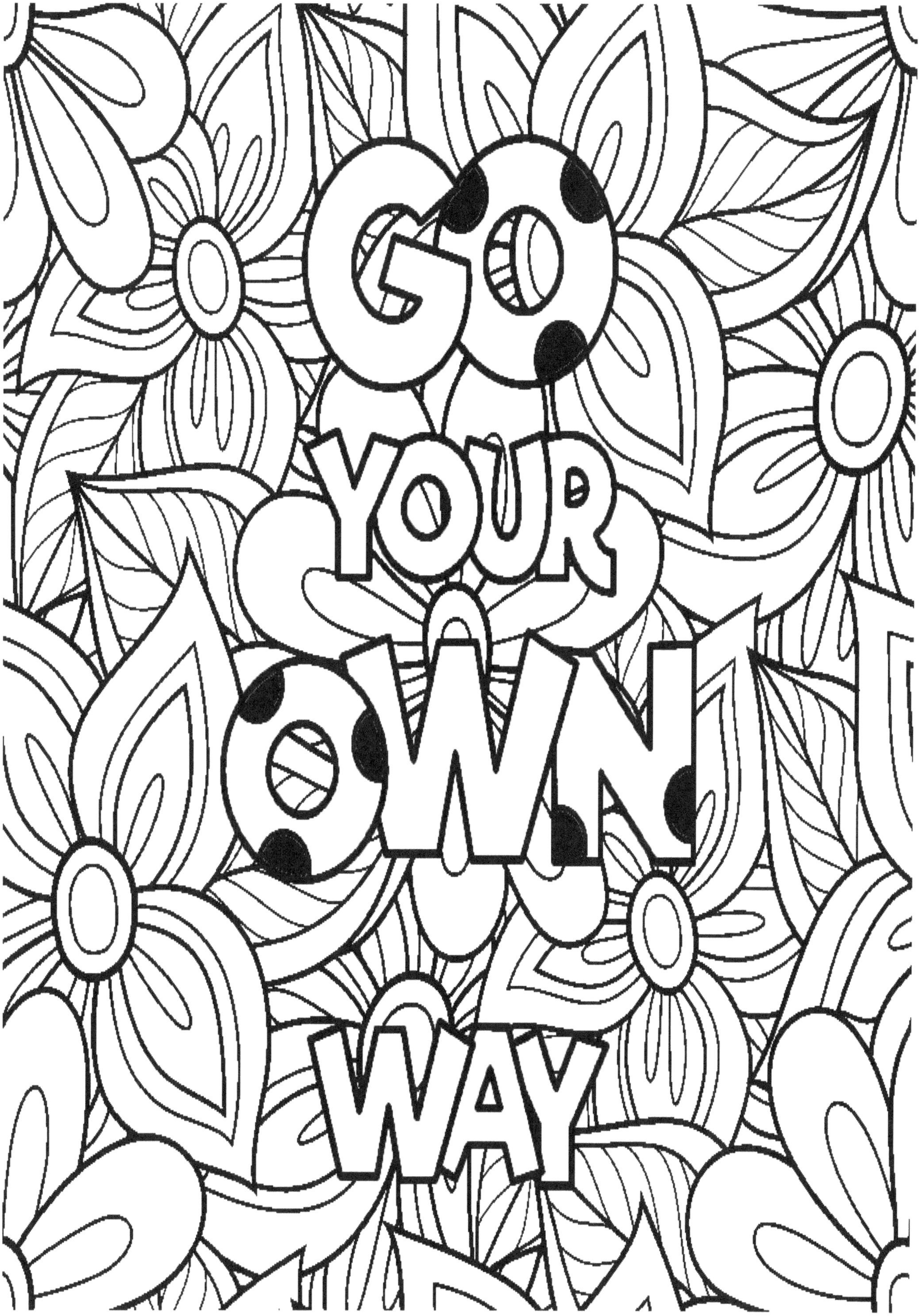
GO
YOUR
OWN
WAY

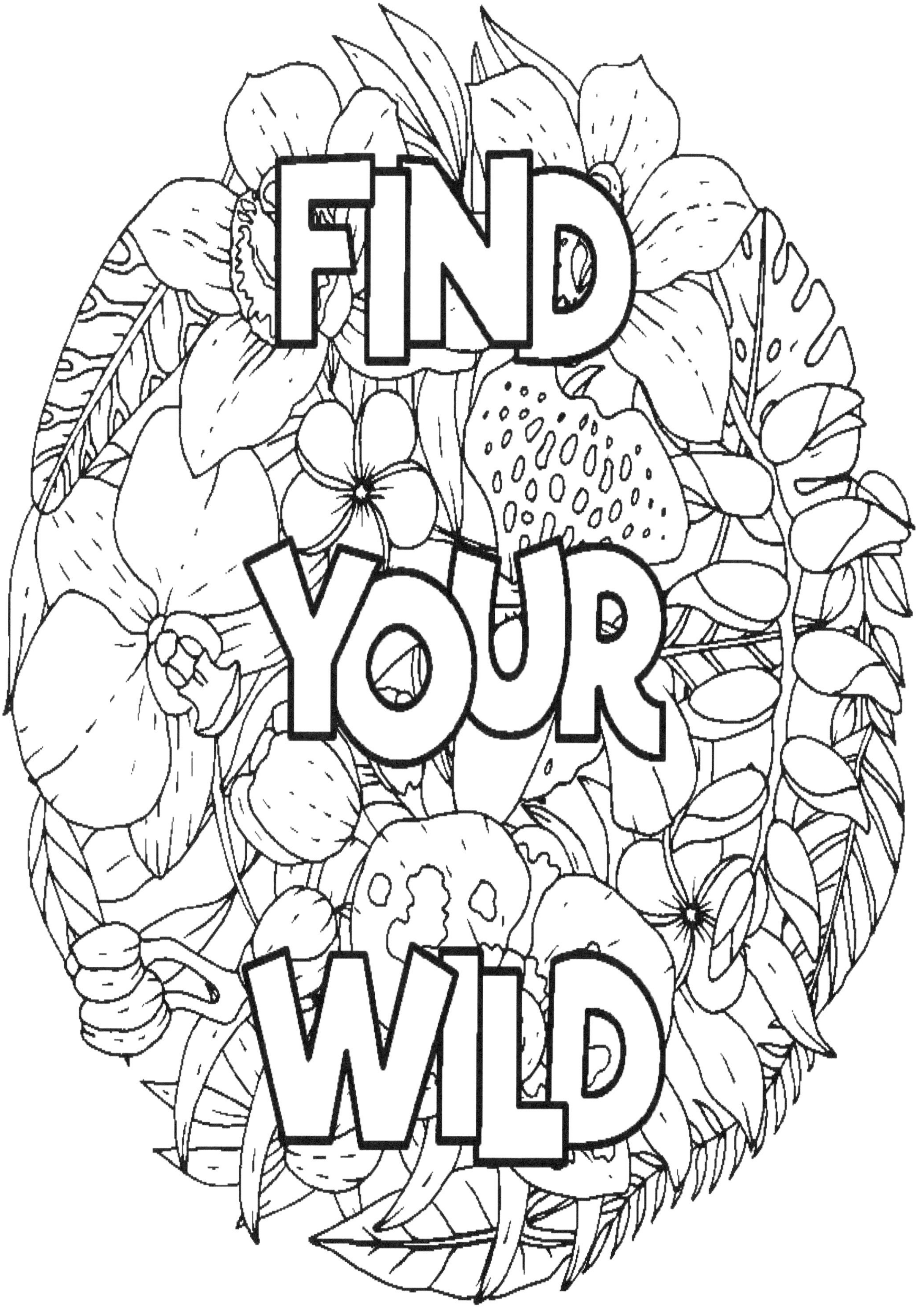
FIND
YOUR
WILD

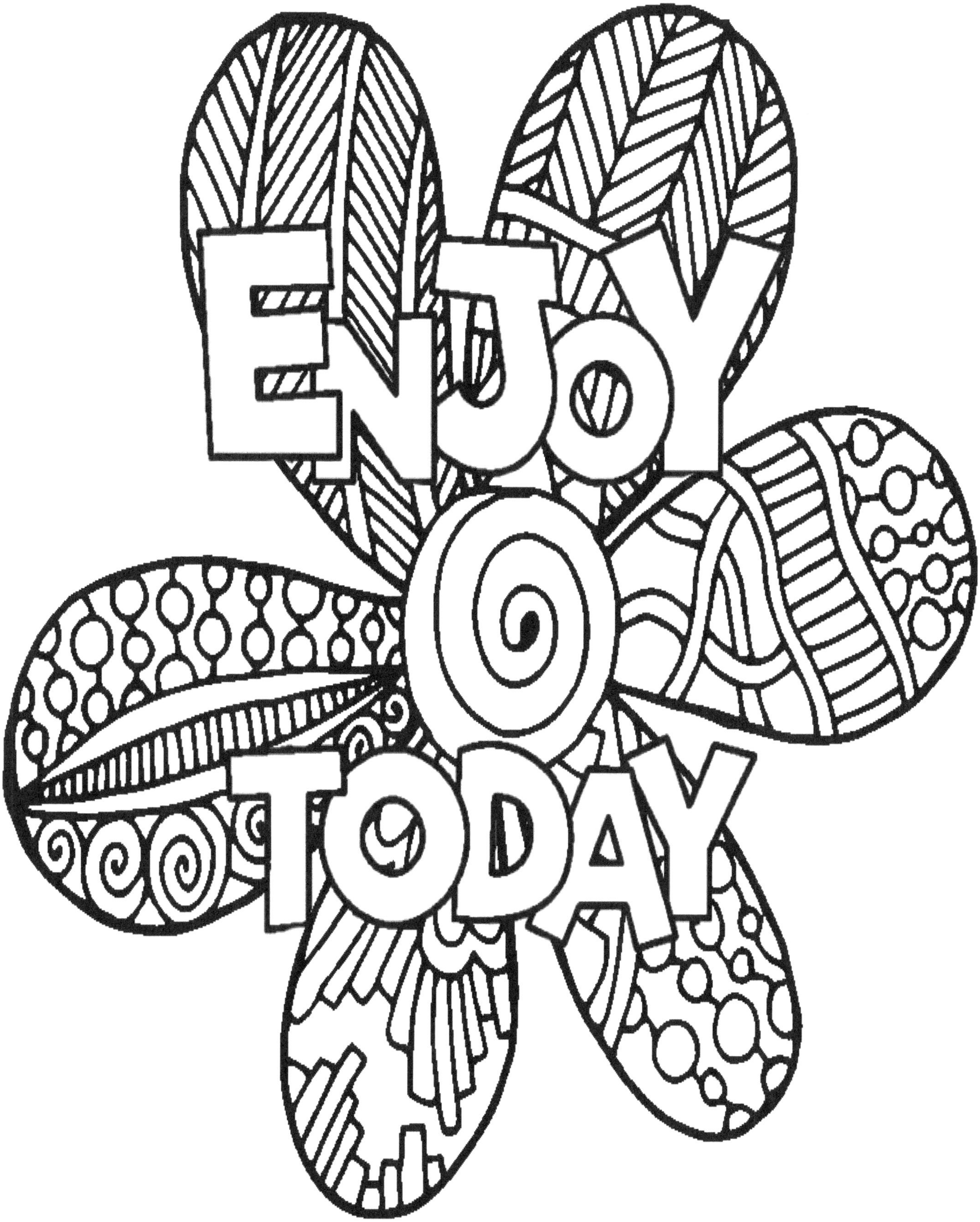
ENJOY
TODAY

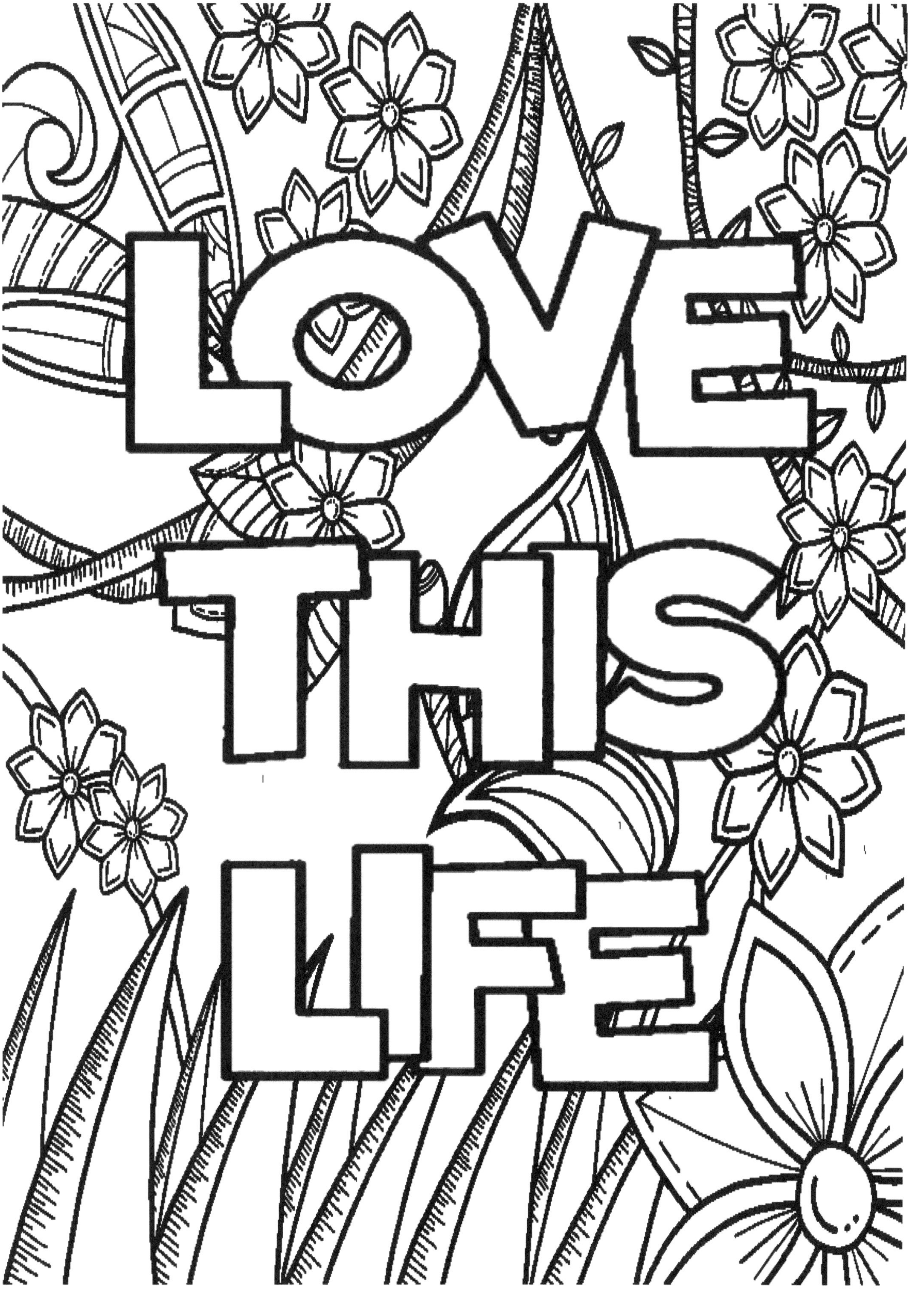
LOVE
THIS
LIFE

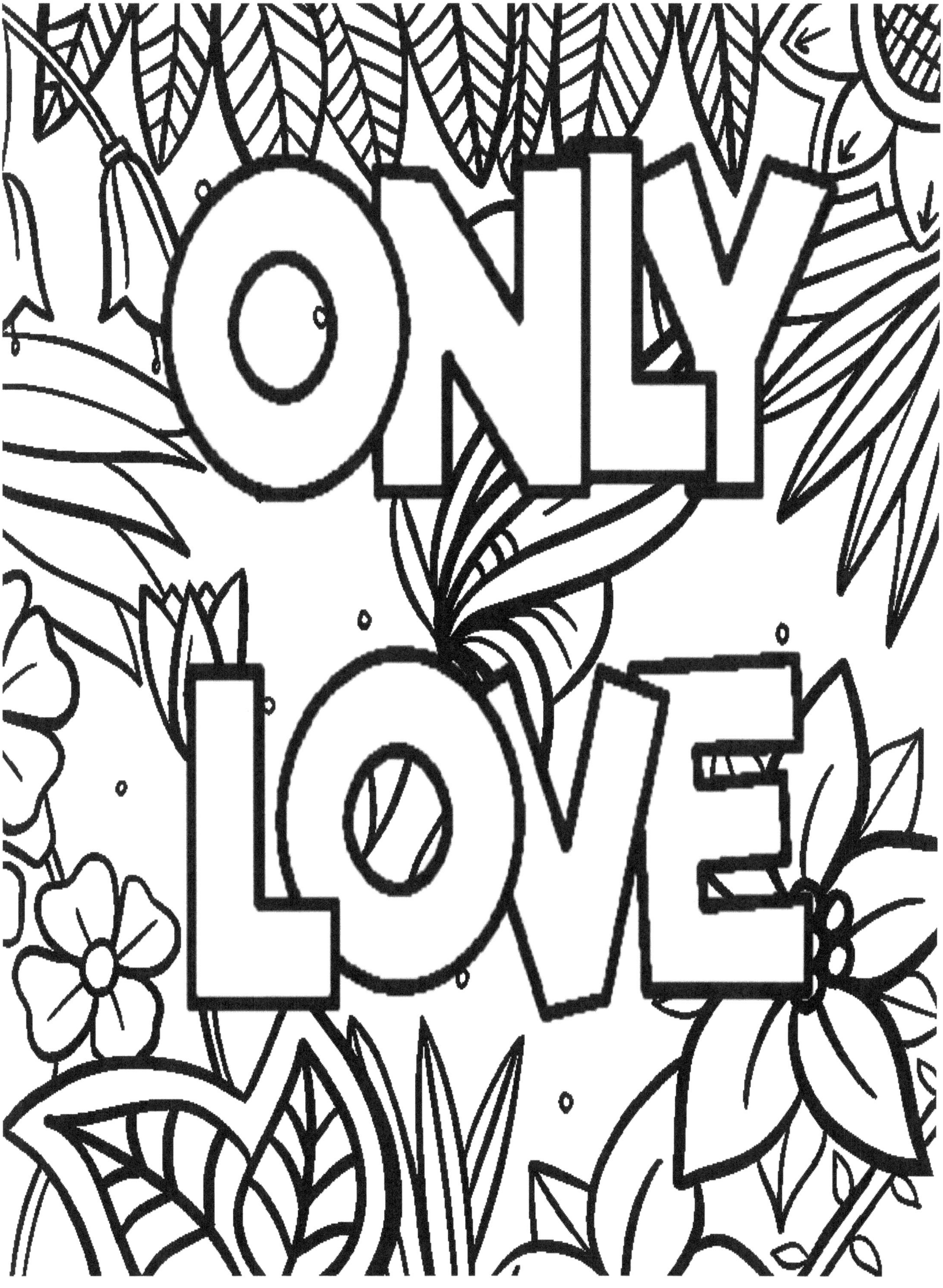
ONLY
LOVE

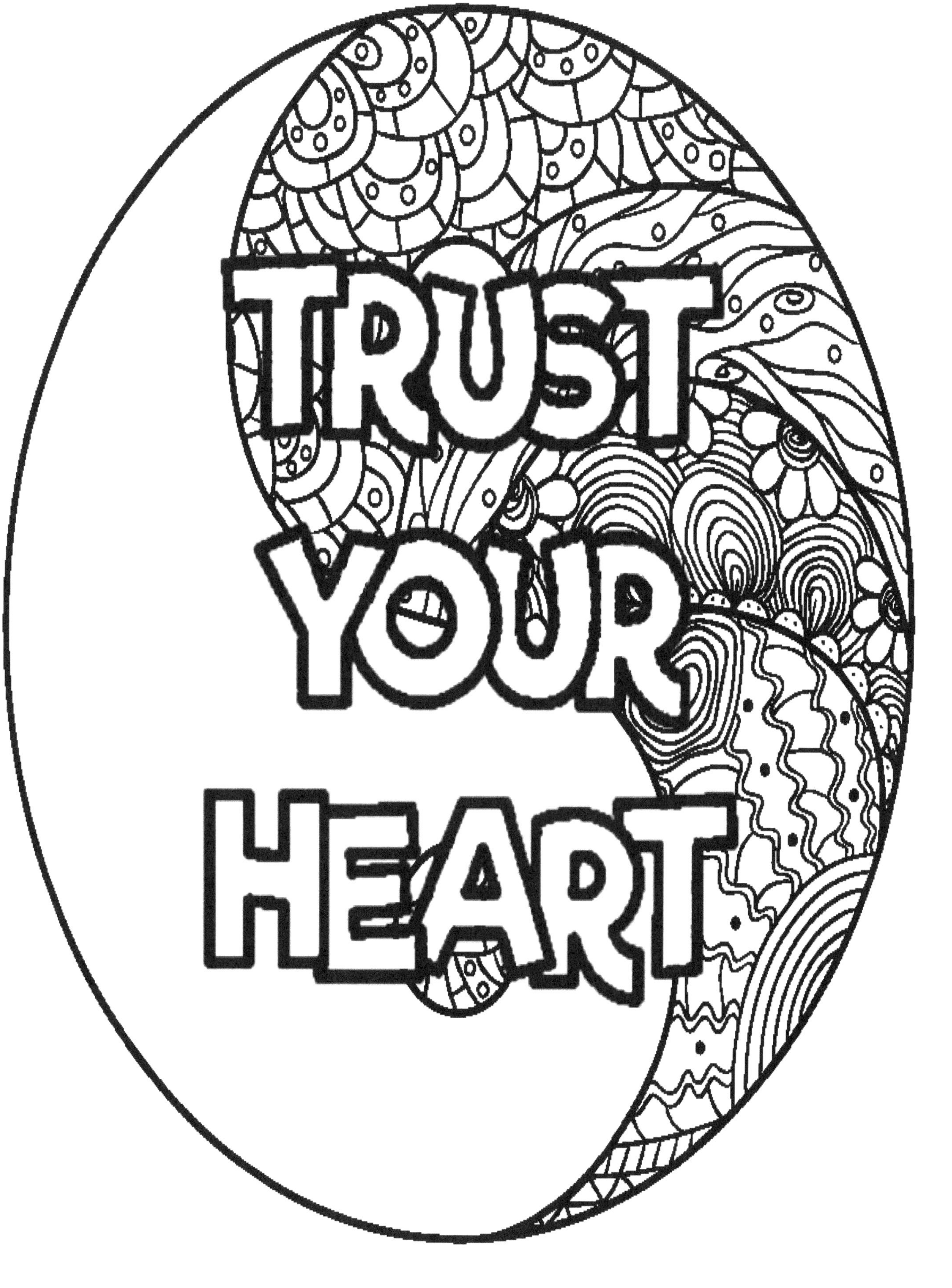
TRUST
YOUR
HEART

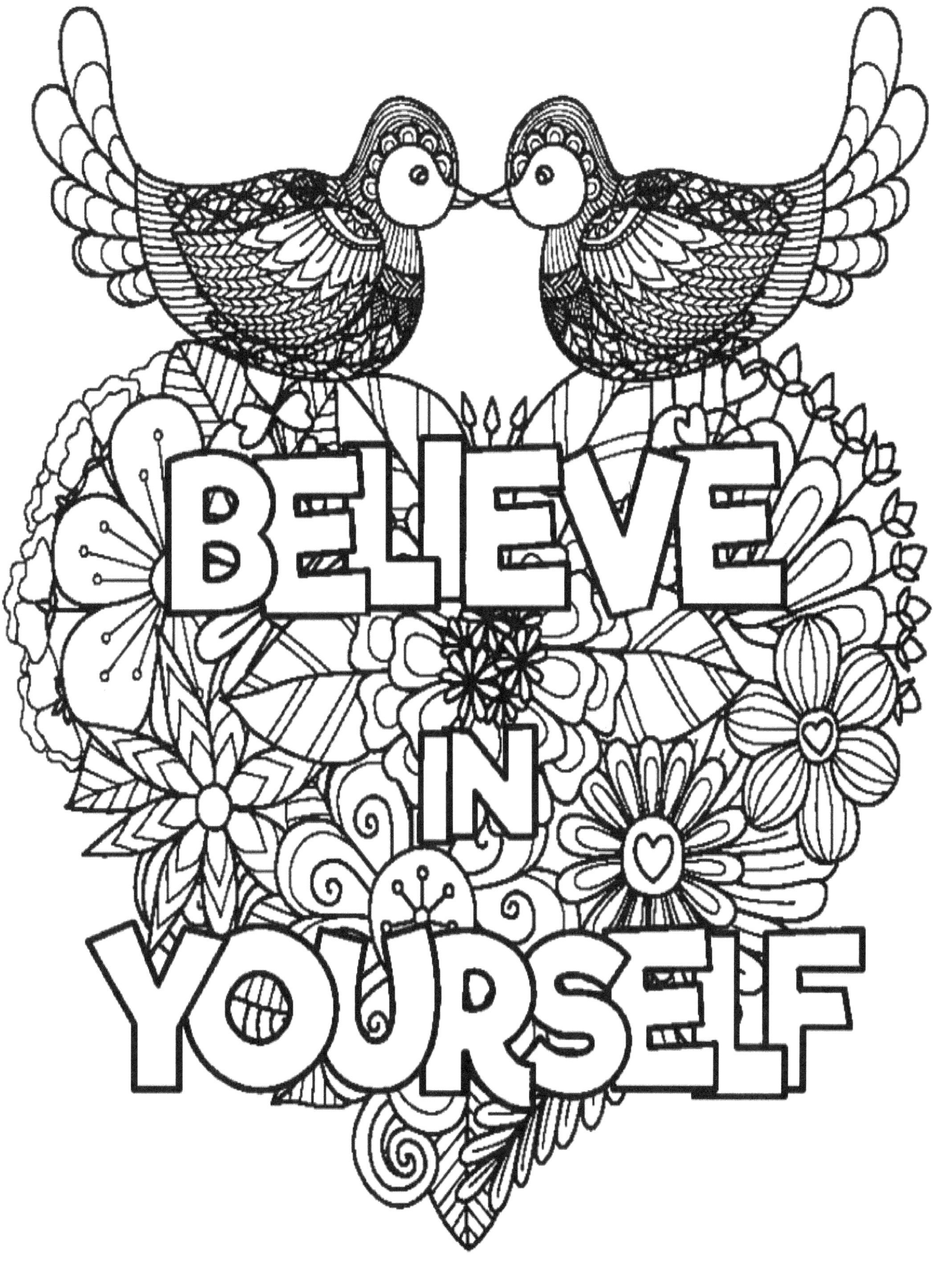
BELIEVE
IN
YOURSELF

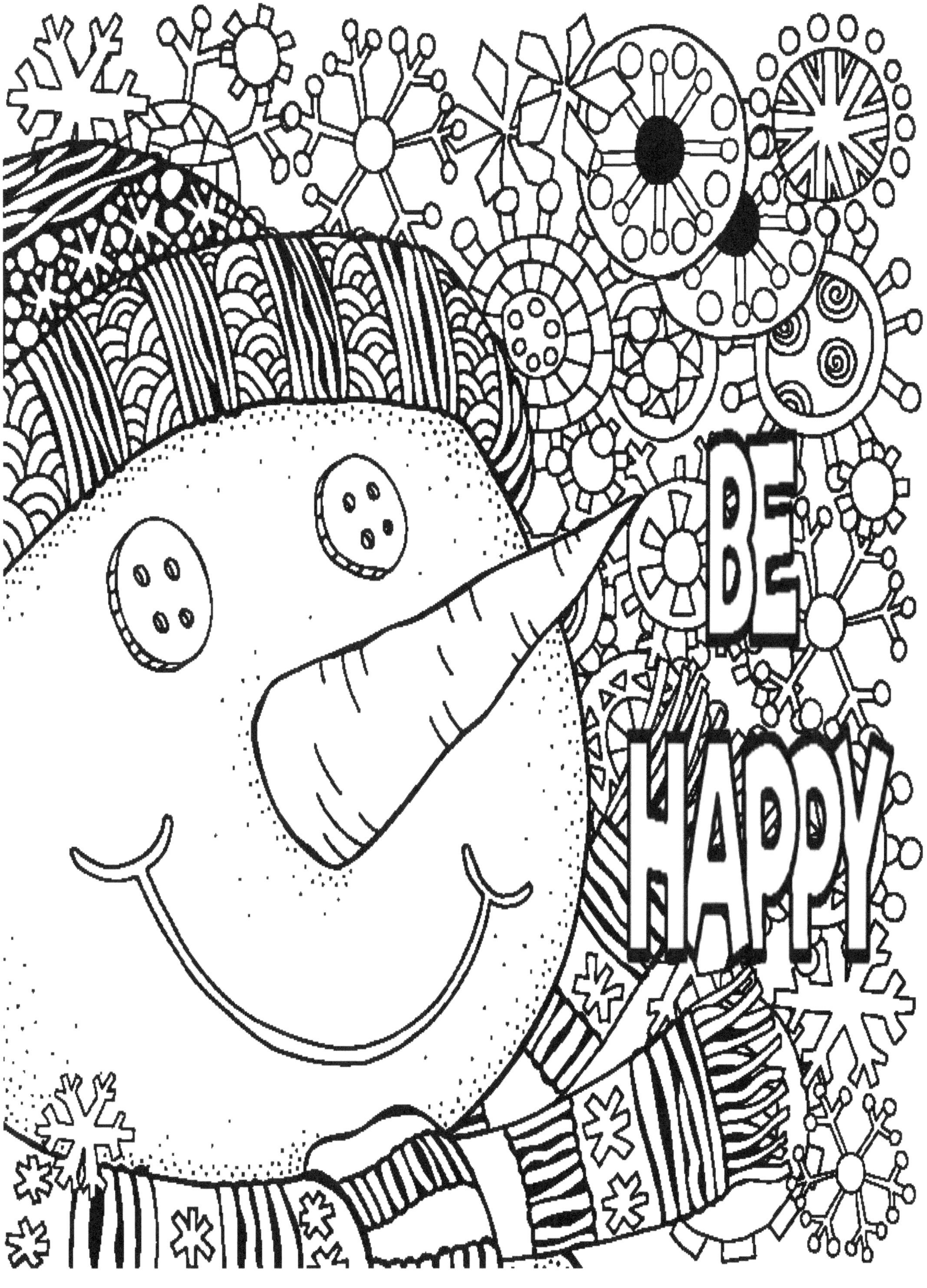
BE
HAPPY

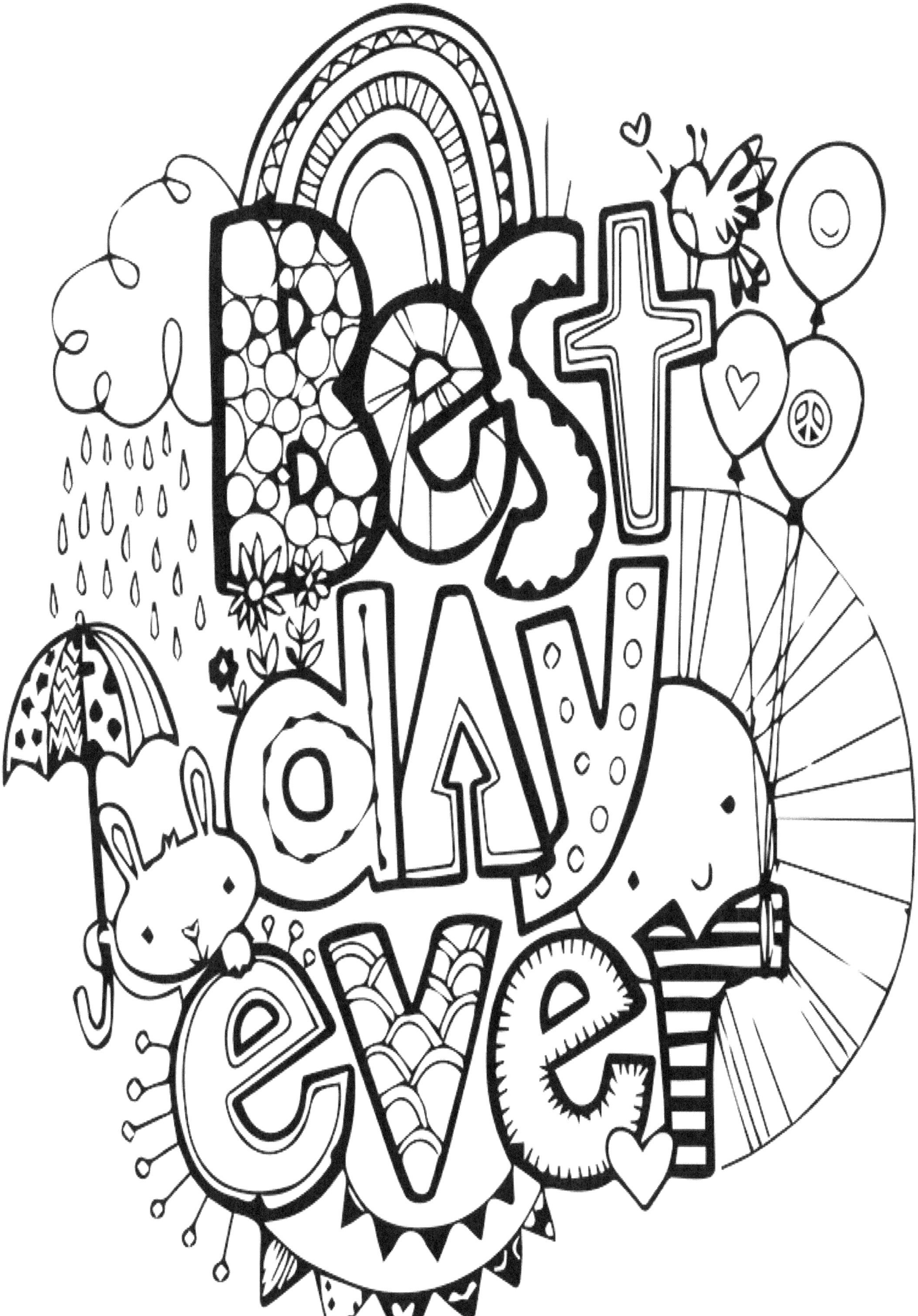
Best
day
ever

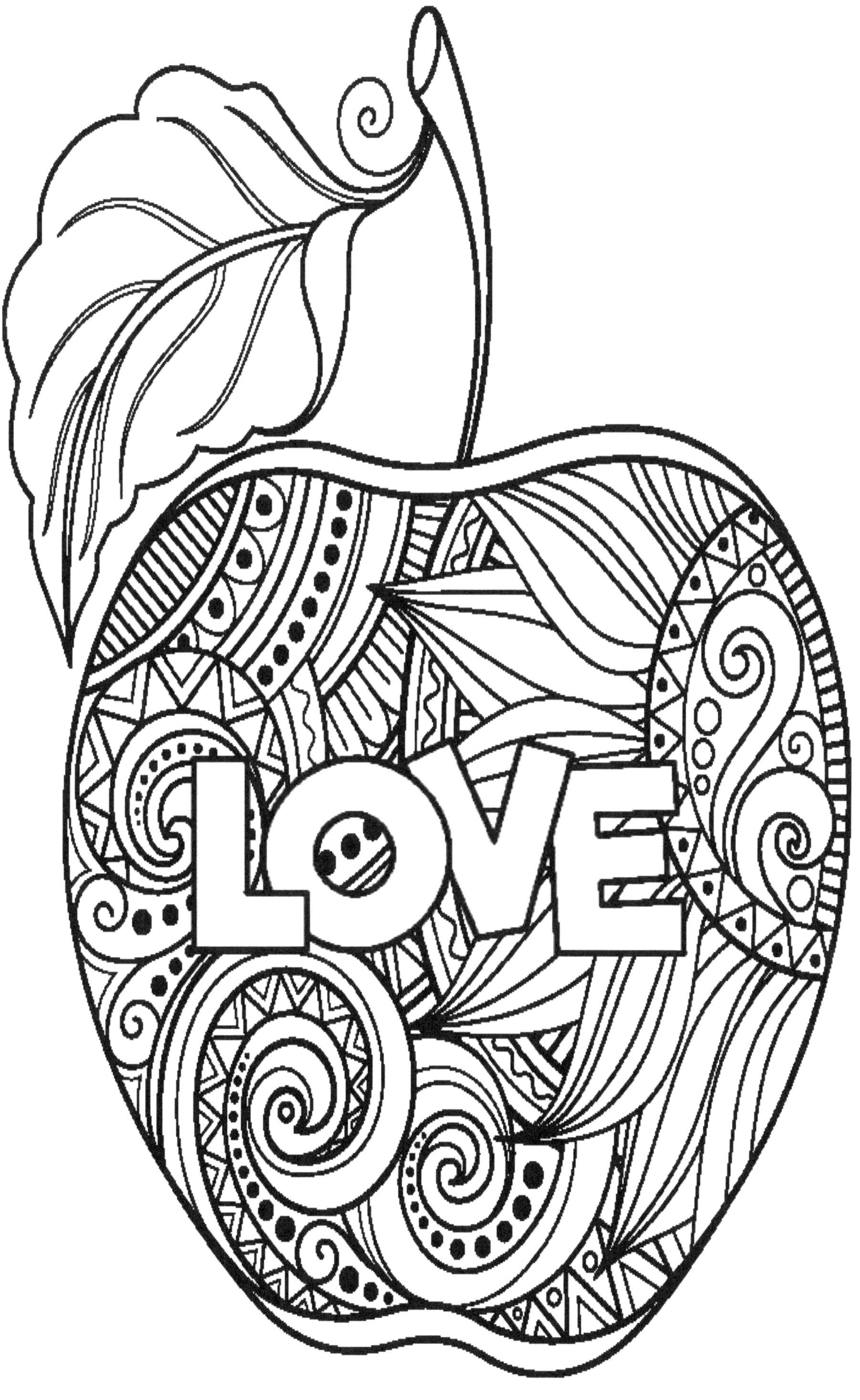
LOVE

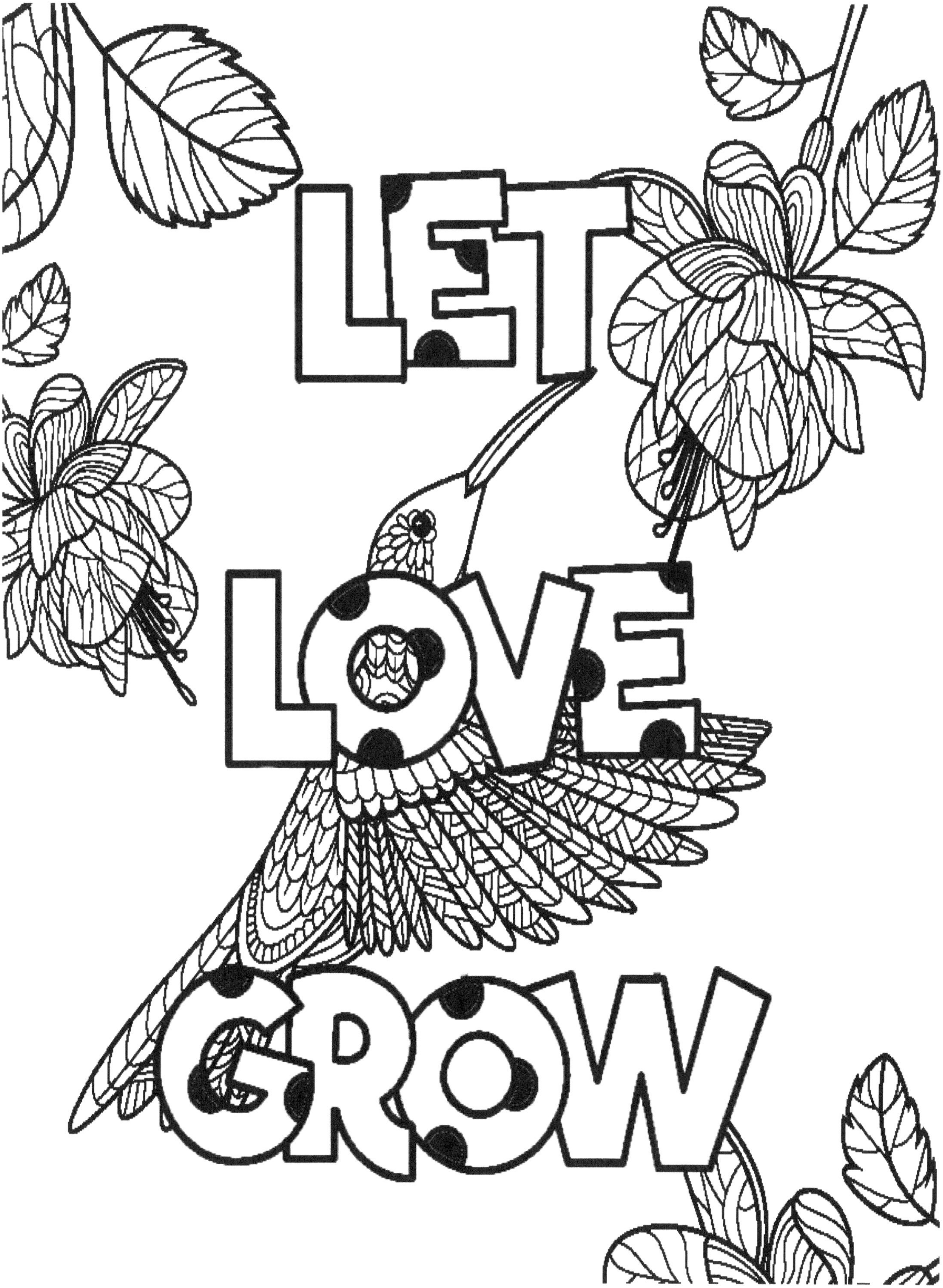
LET
LOVE
GROW

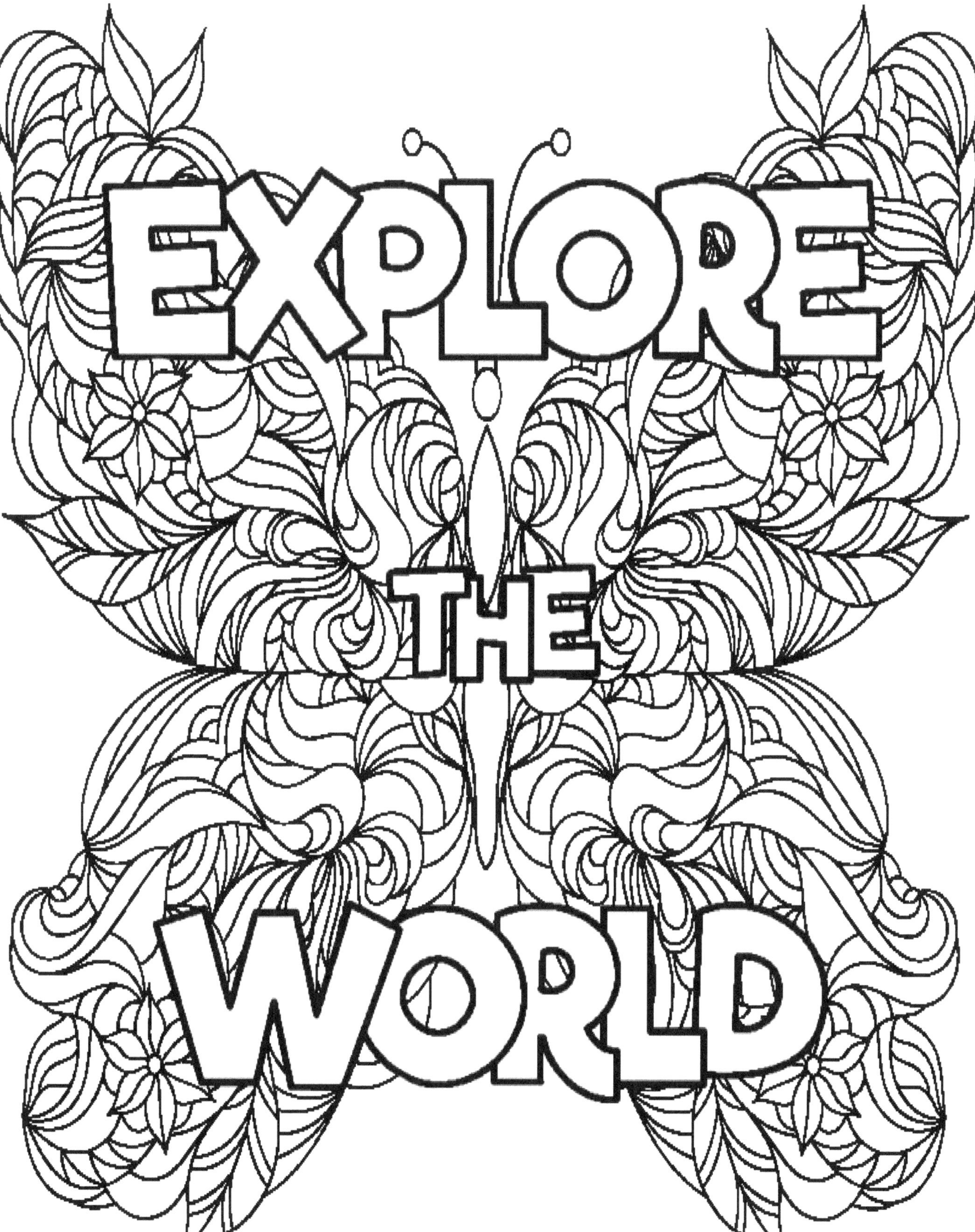
EXPLORE
THE
WORLD

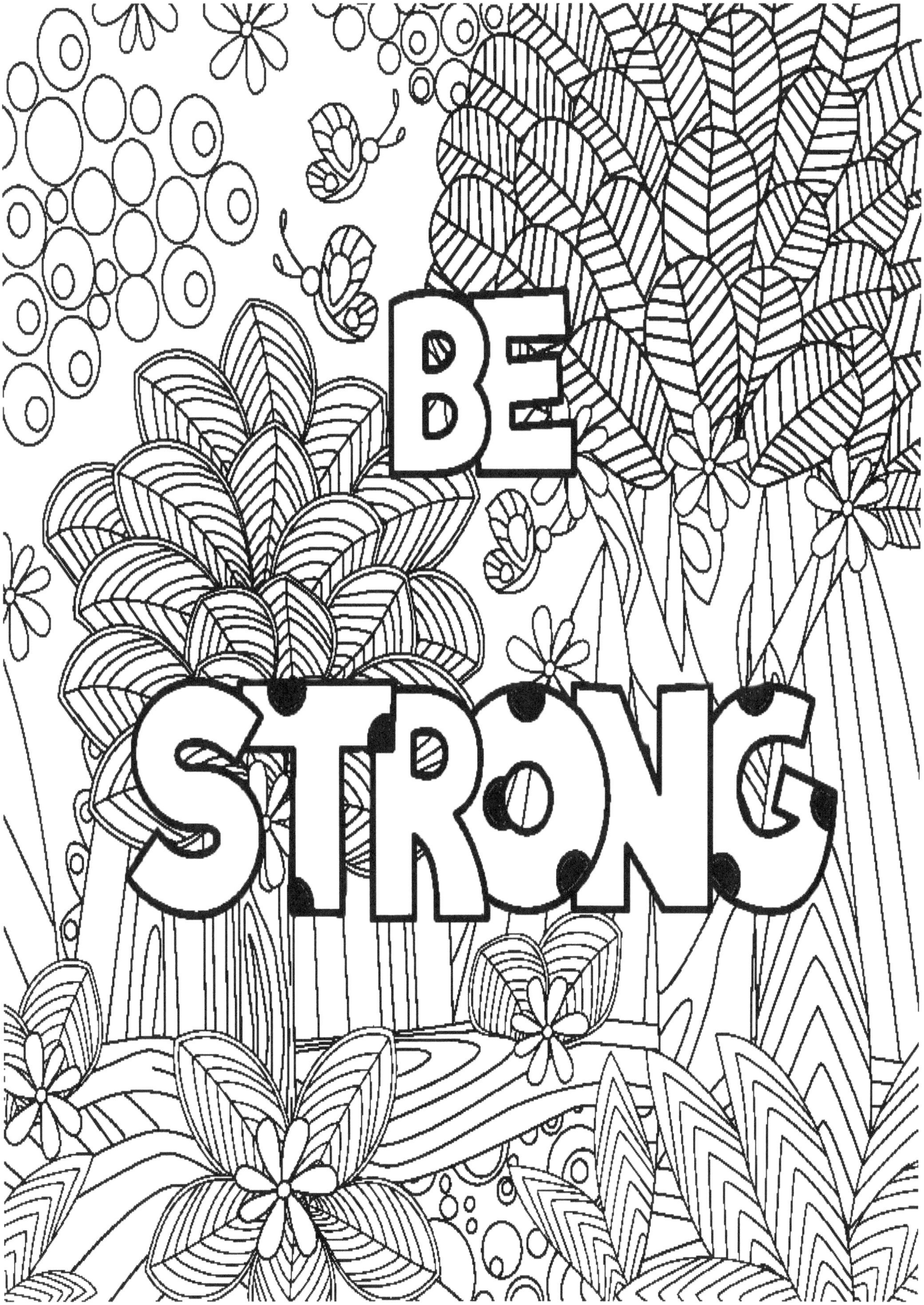
BE
STRONG

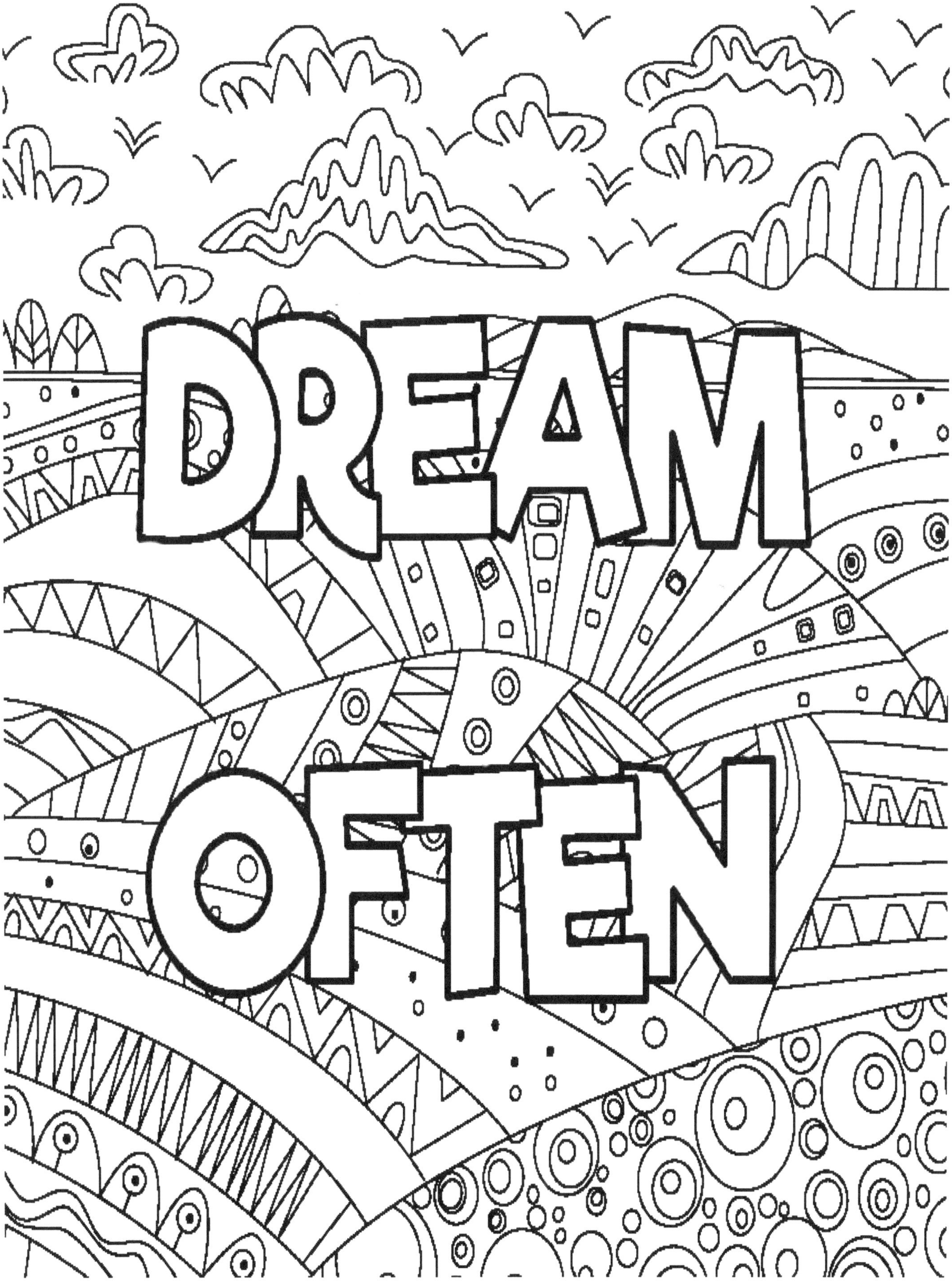
DREAM
OFTEN

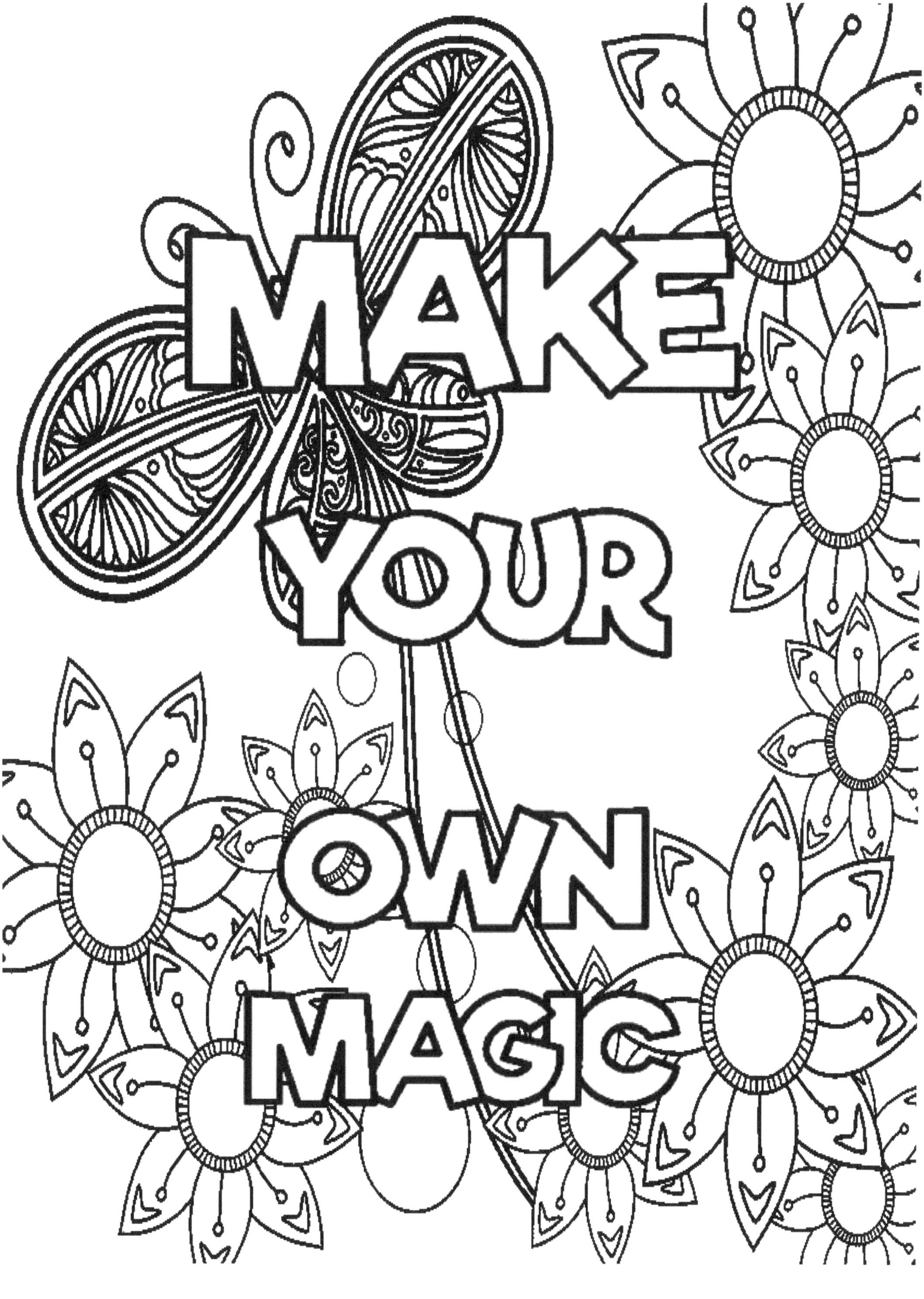
MAKE
YOUR
OWN
MAGIC

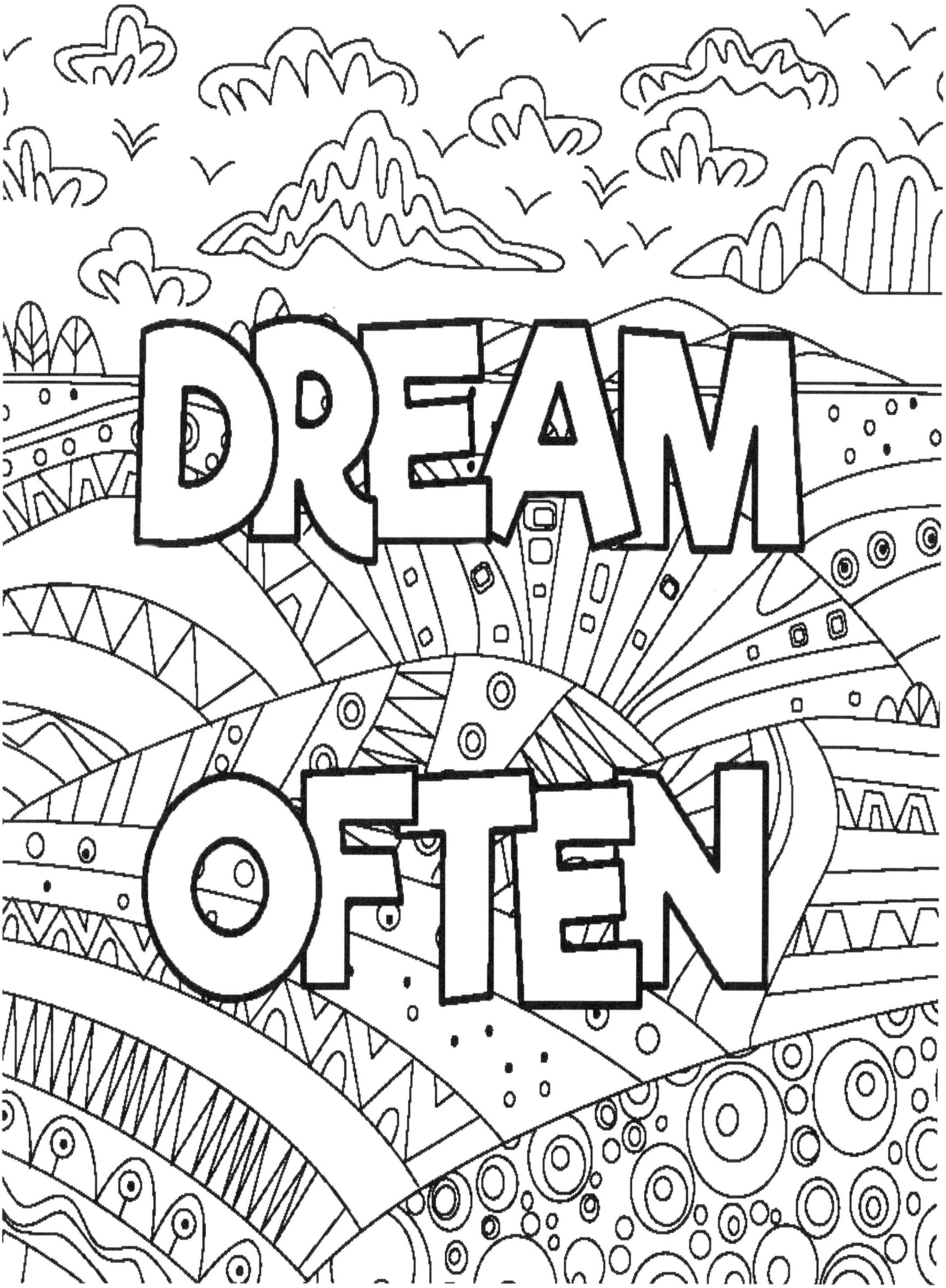
DREAM
OFTEN

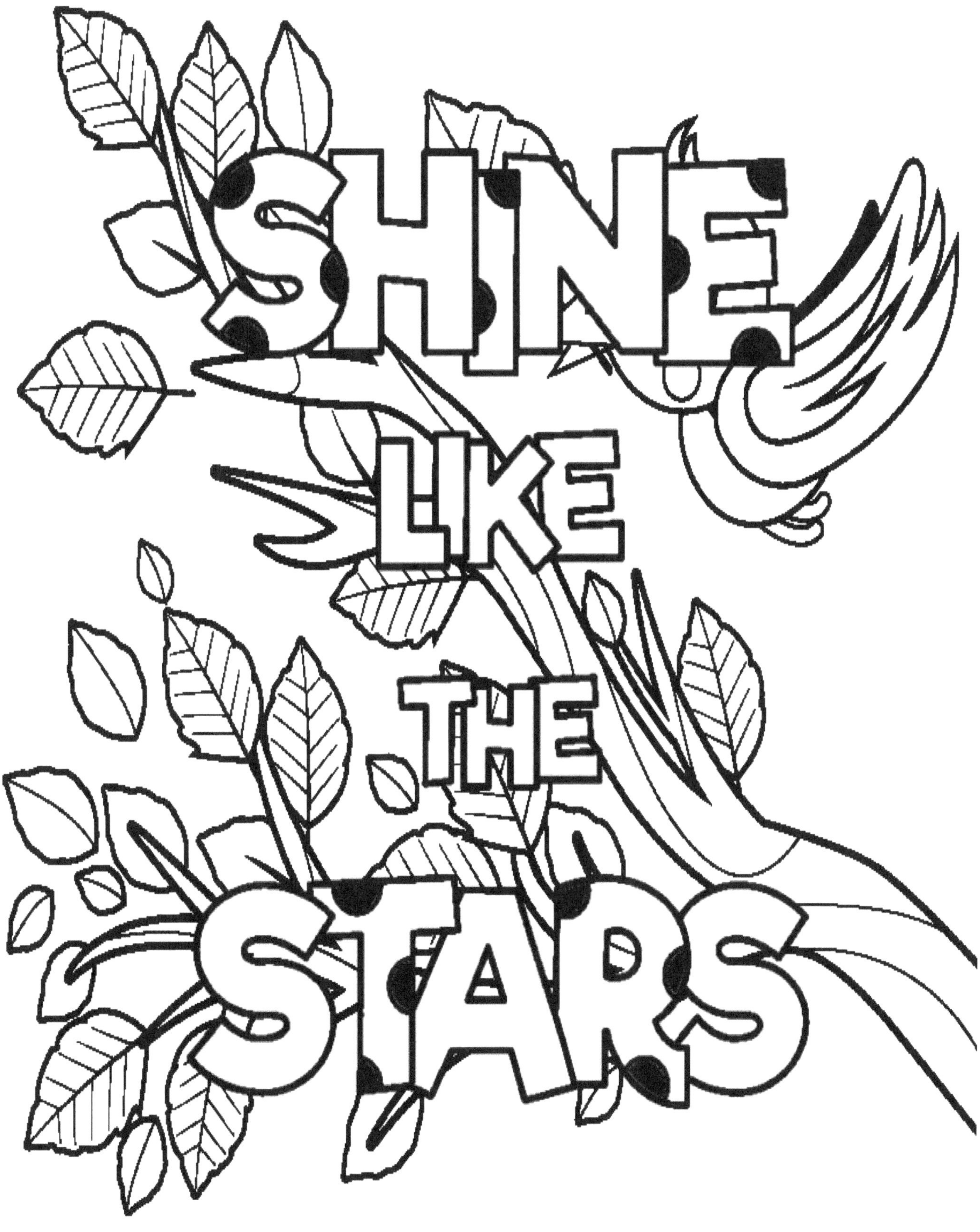
SHINE
LIKE
THE
STARS

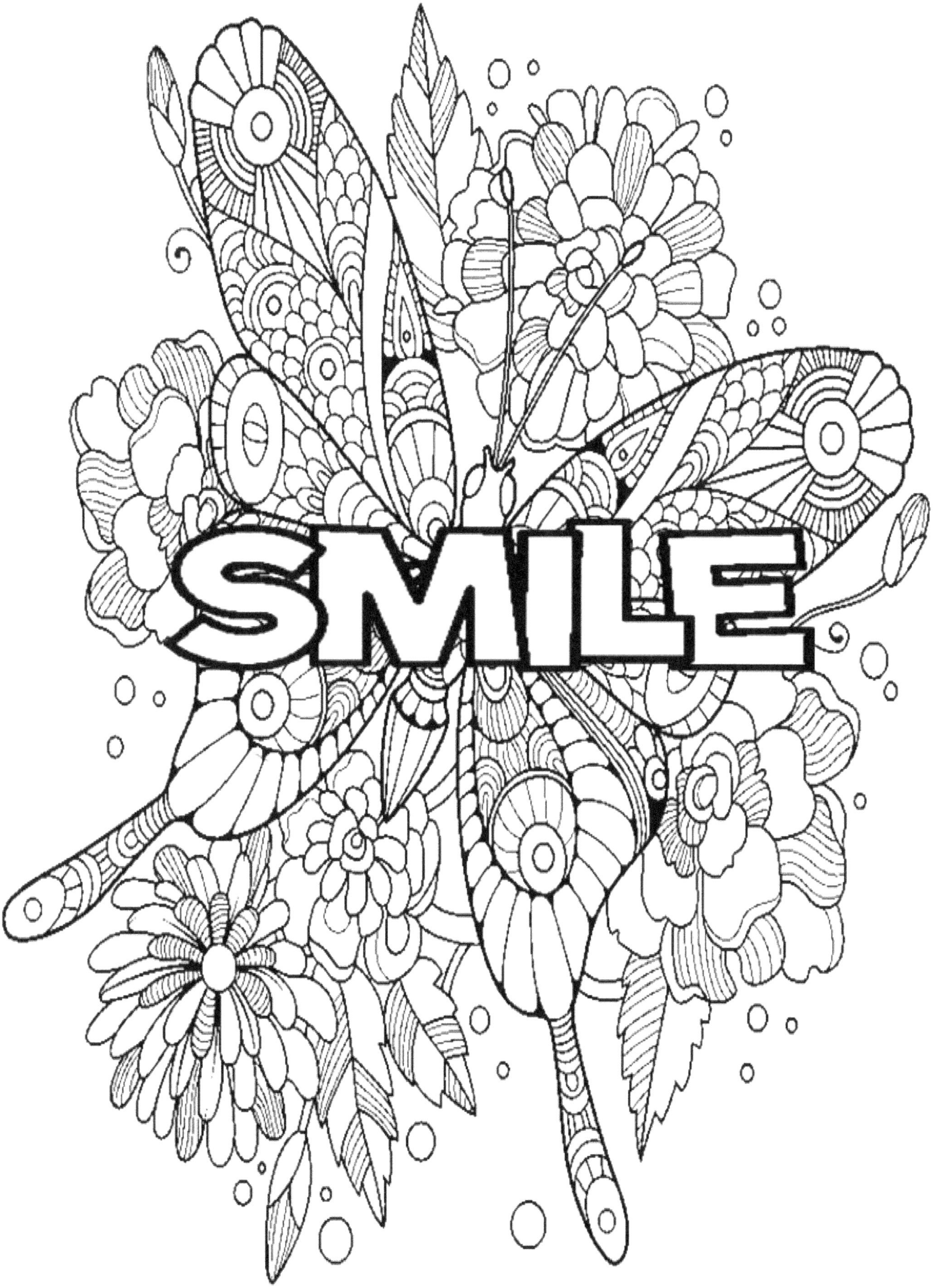
SMILE

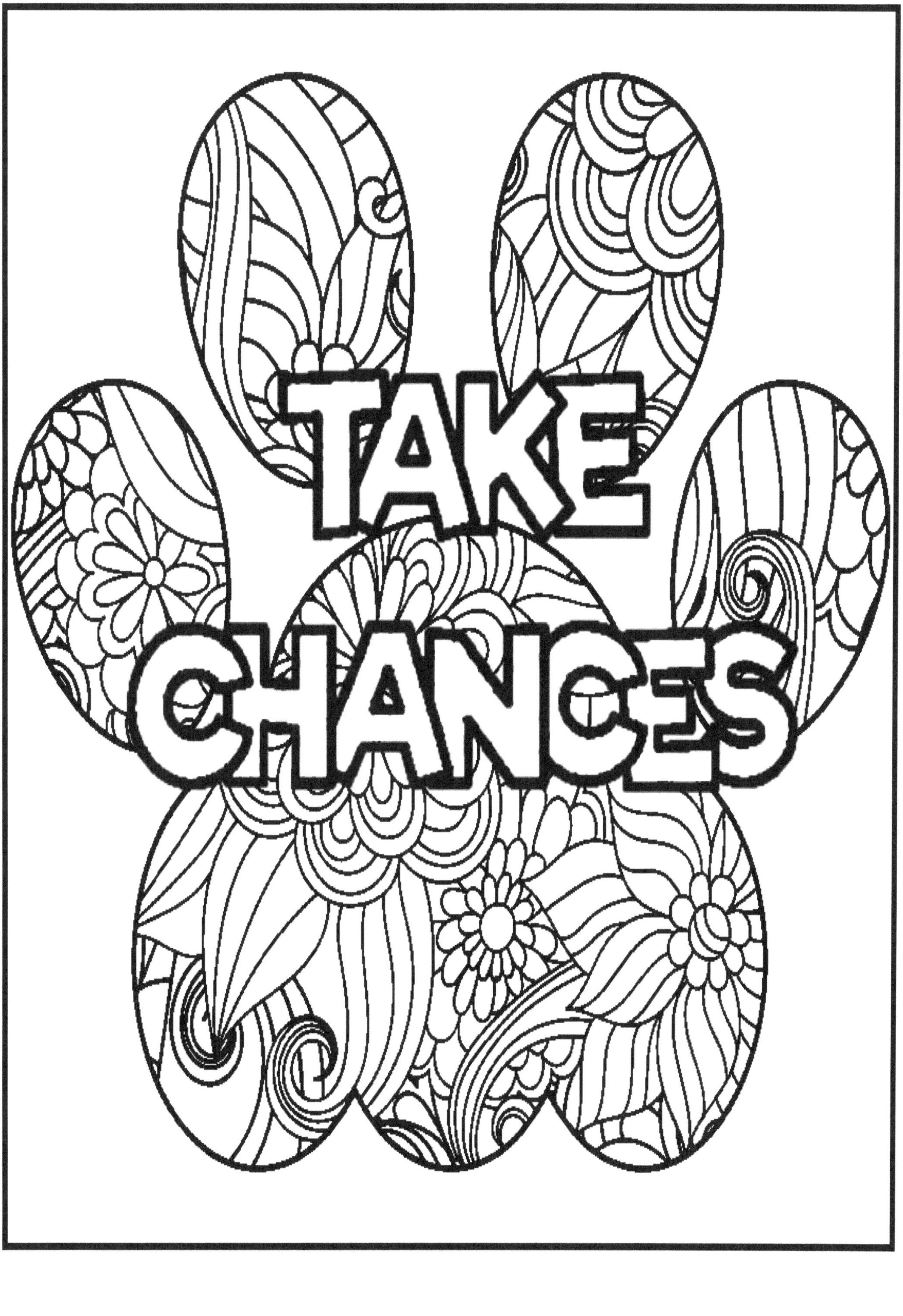
TAKE
CHANCES

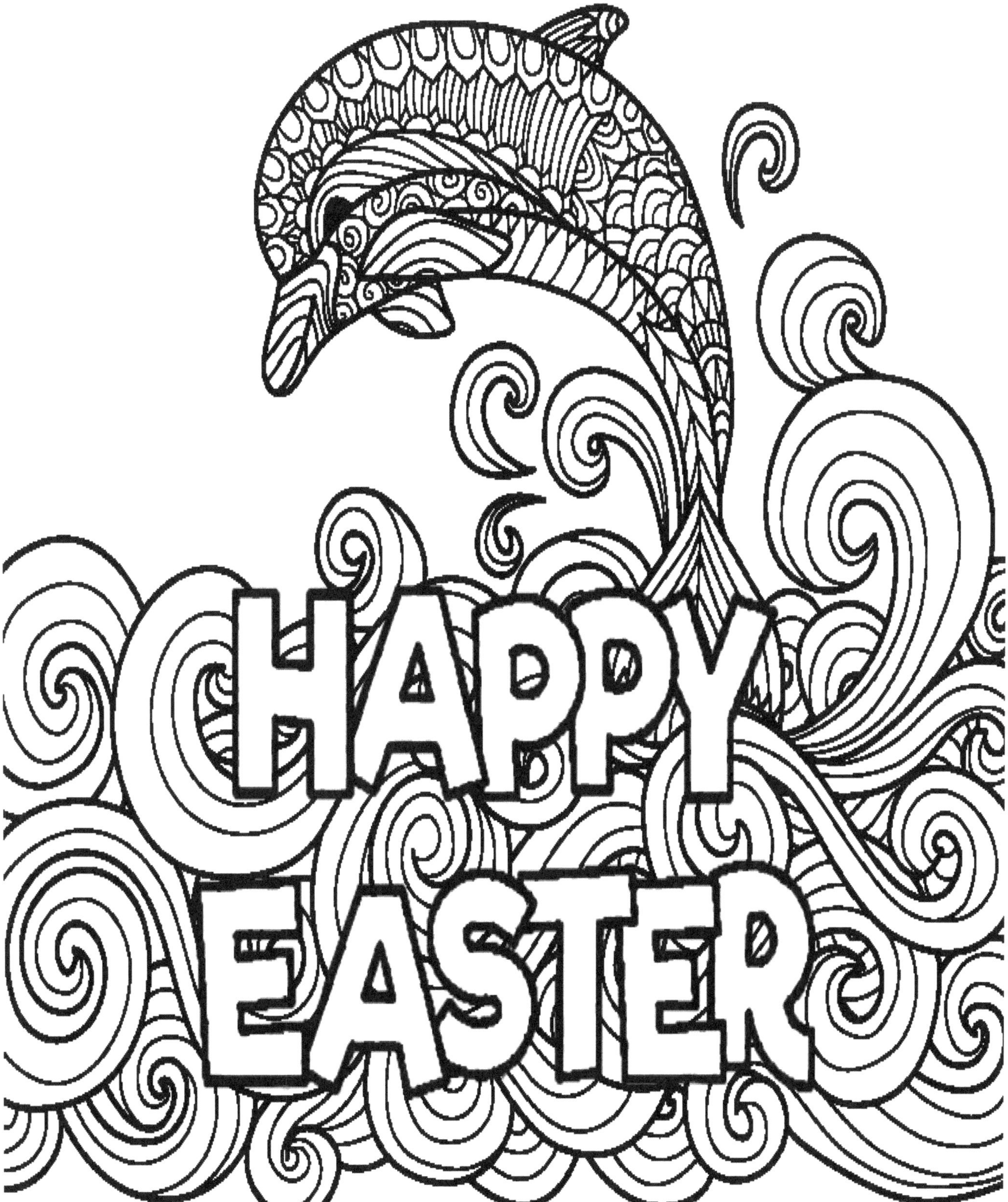
HAPPY
EASTER

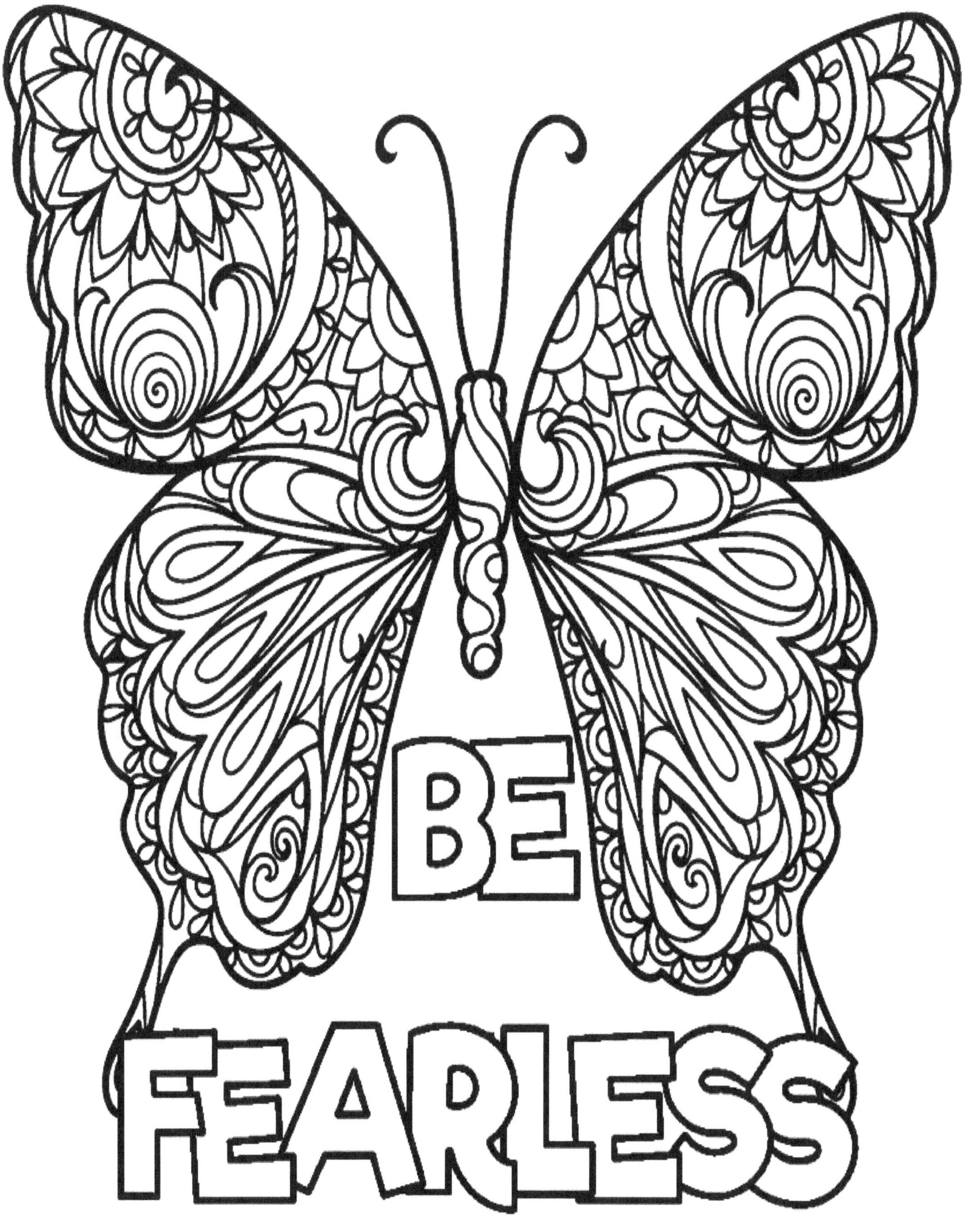
BE
FEARLESS

OPEN
YOUR
HEART

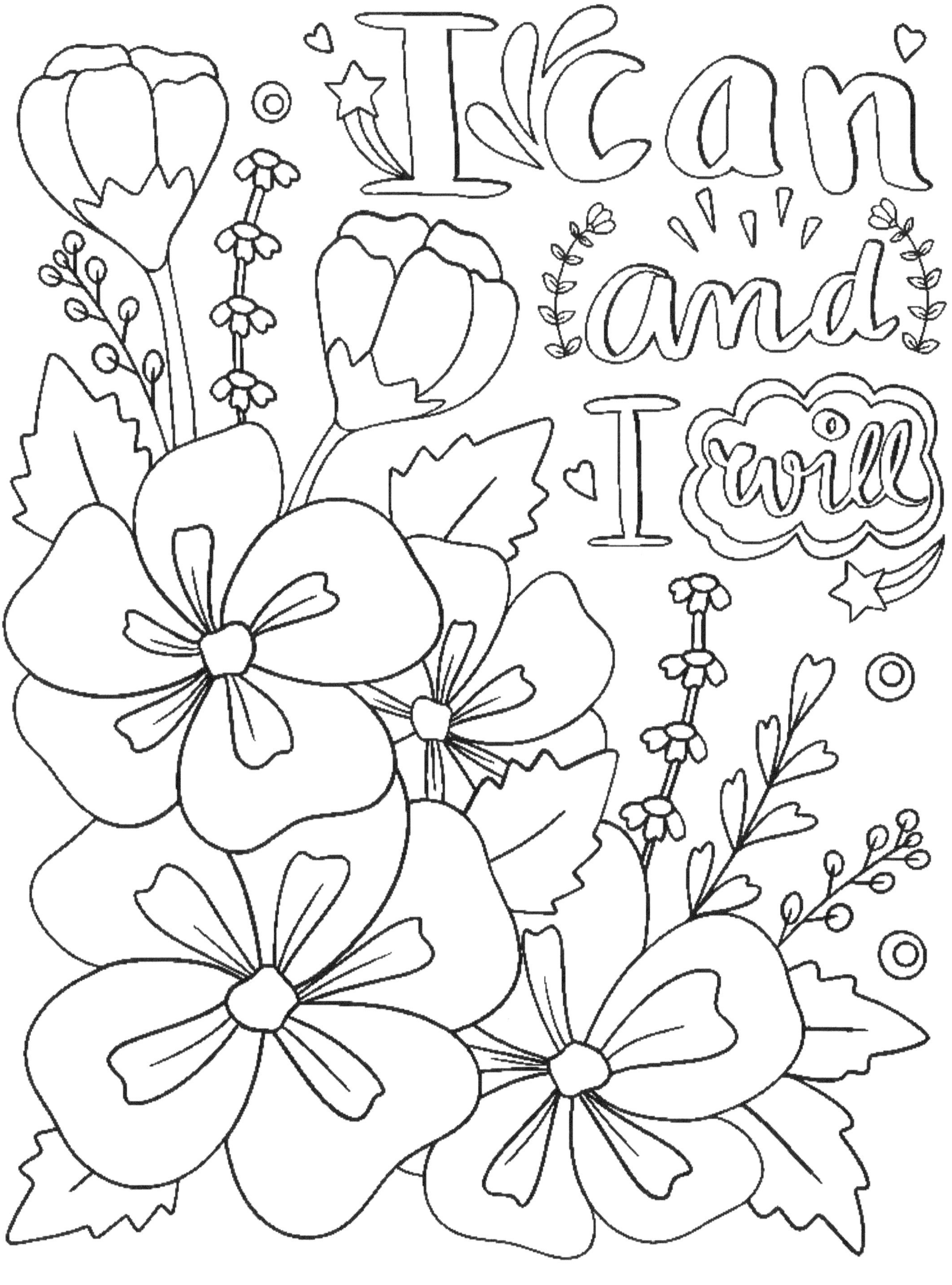
I can and I will

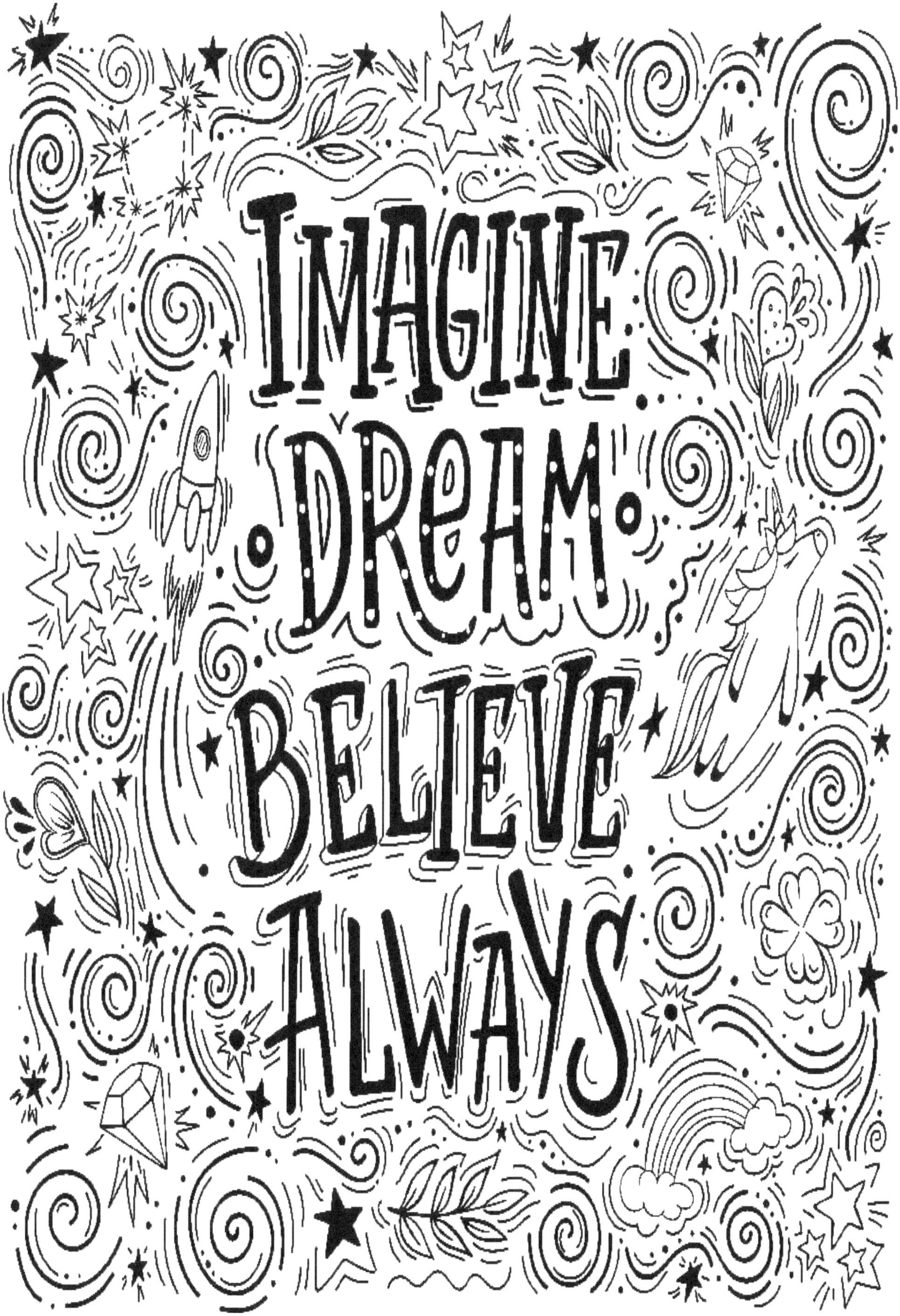
IMAGINE
DREAM
BELIEVE
ALWAYS

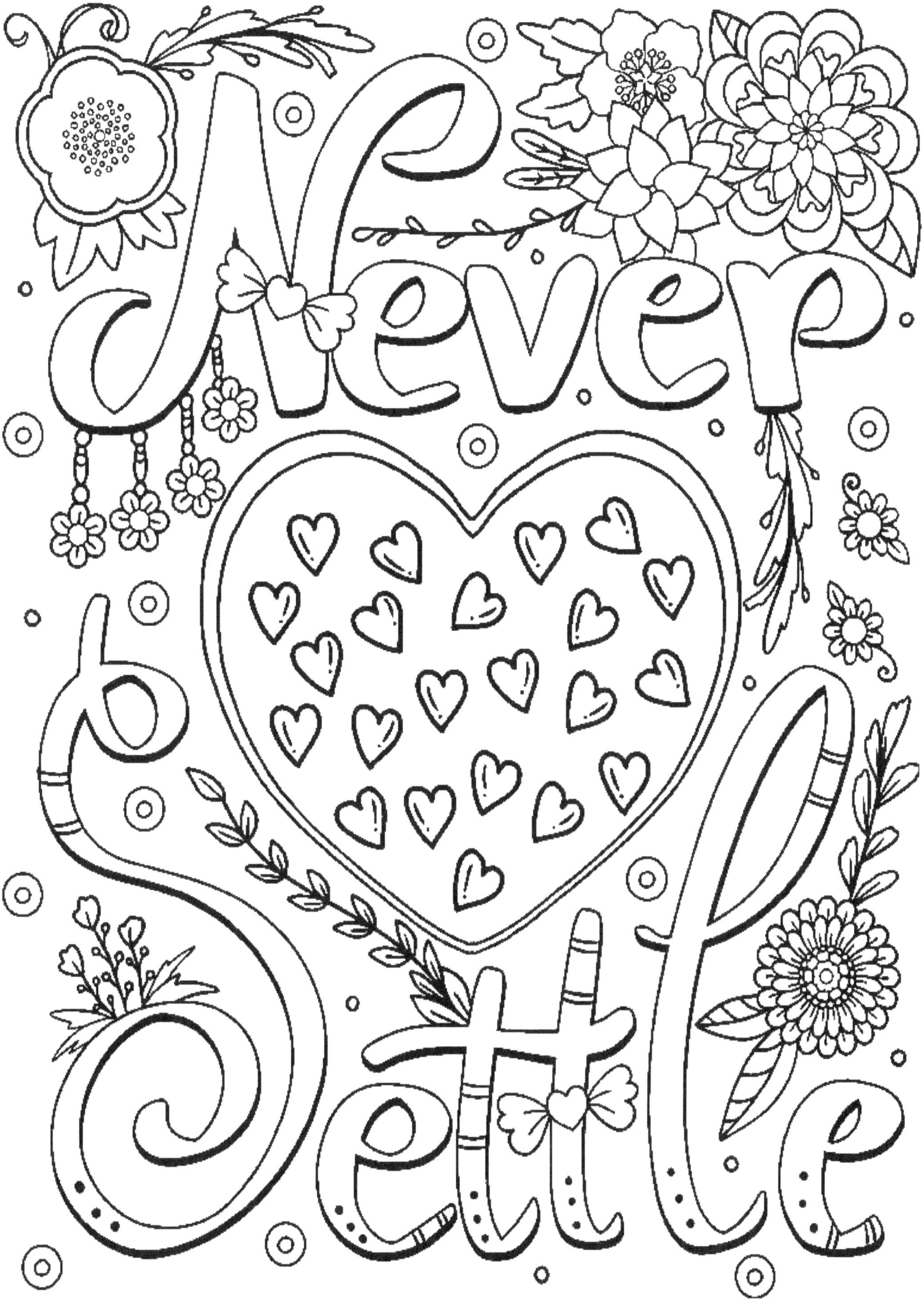
Never
Settle

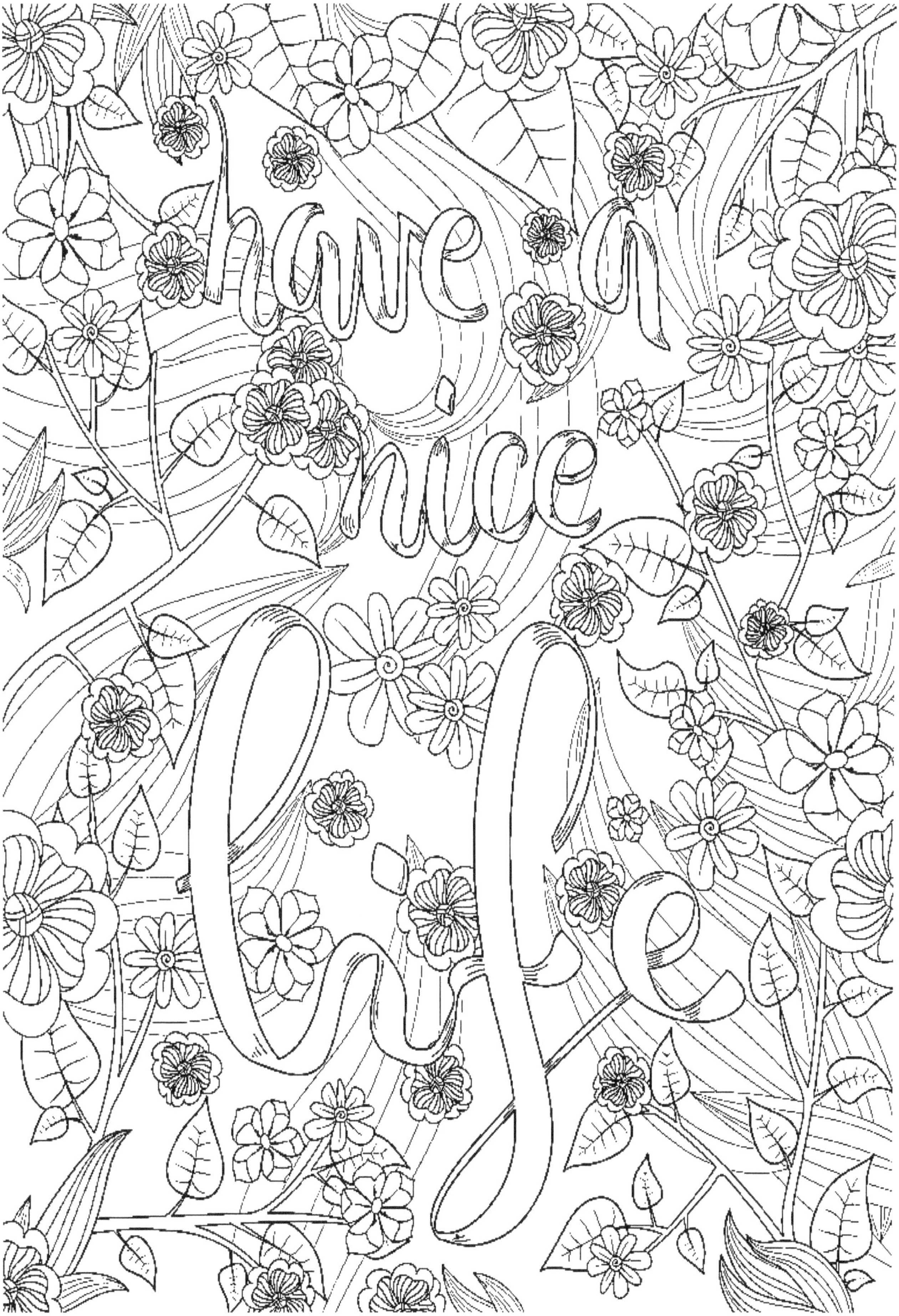
have a nice life

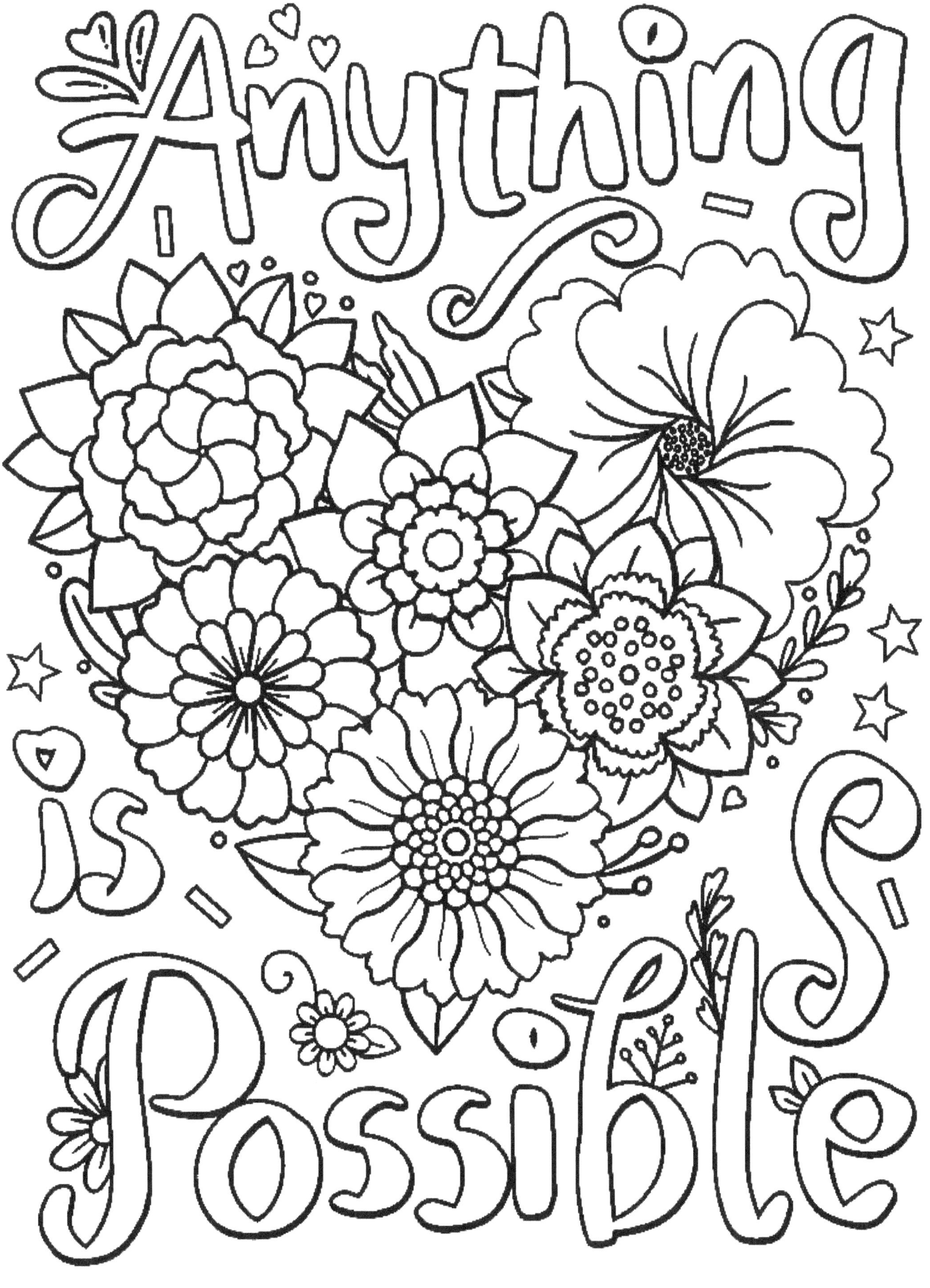
Anything
is
Possible

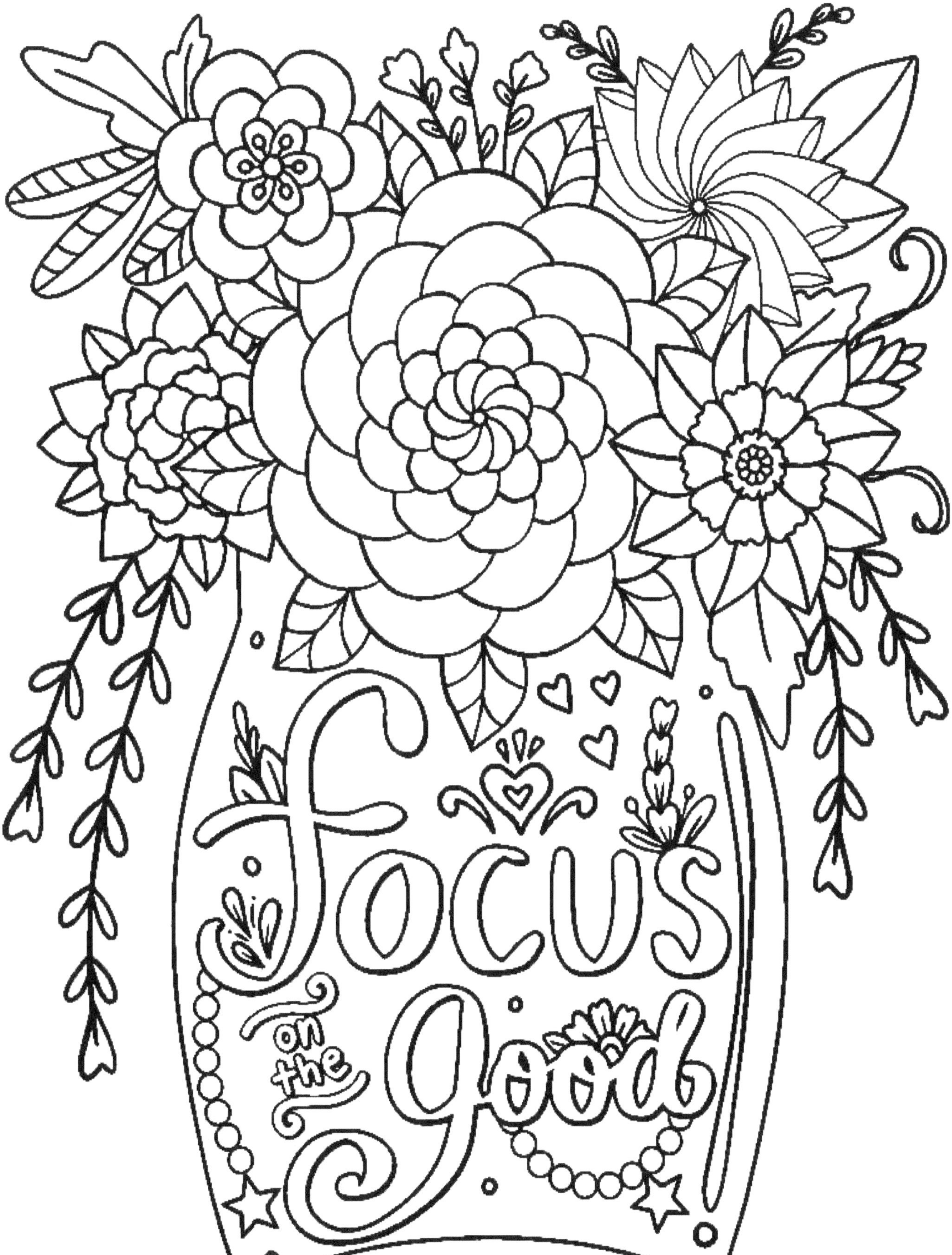
Focus
on the
good

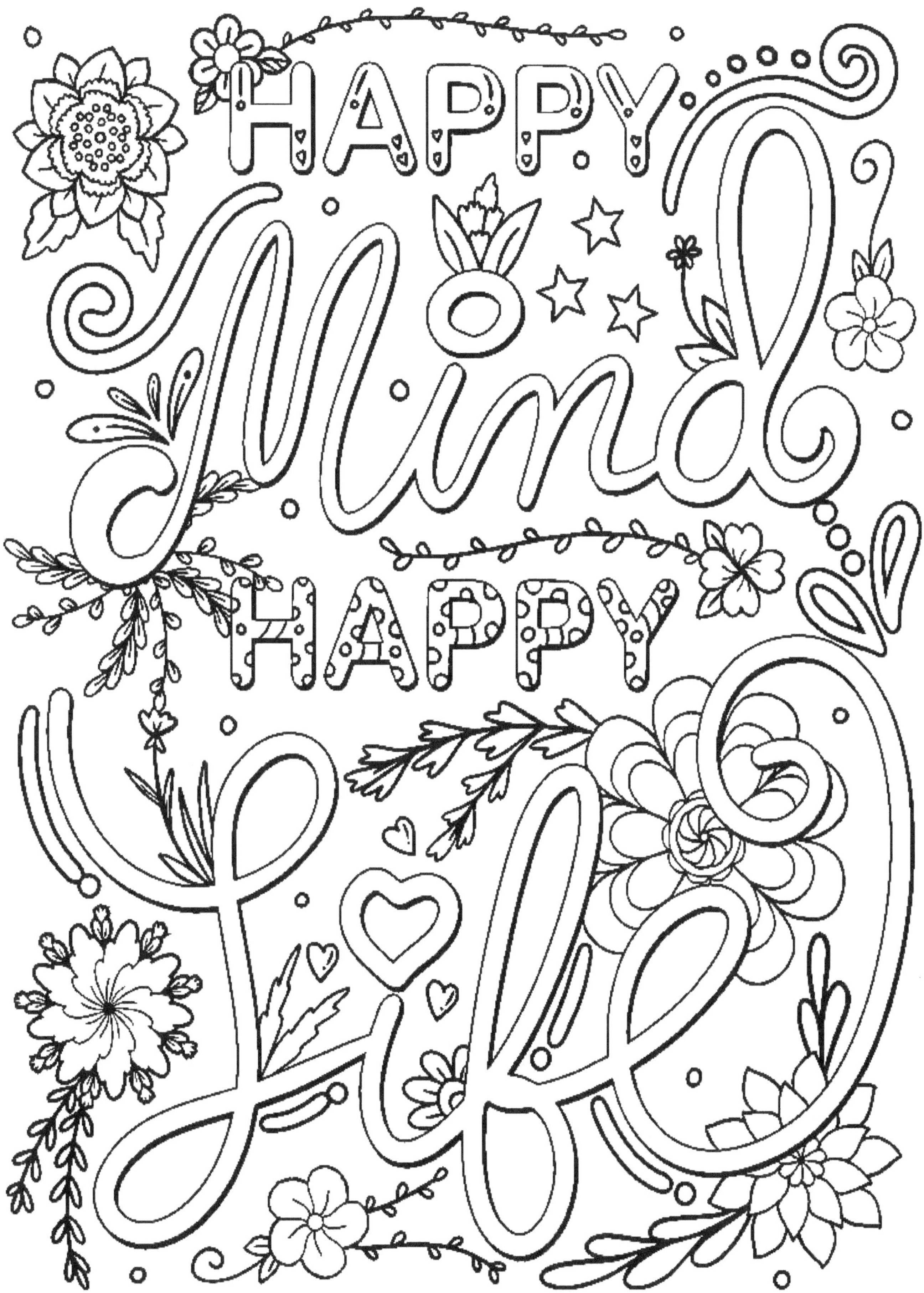
HAPPY
Mind
HAPPY
Life

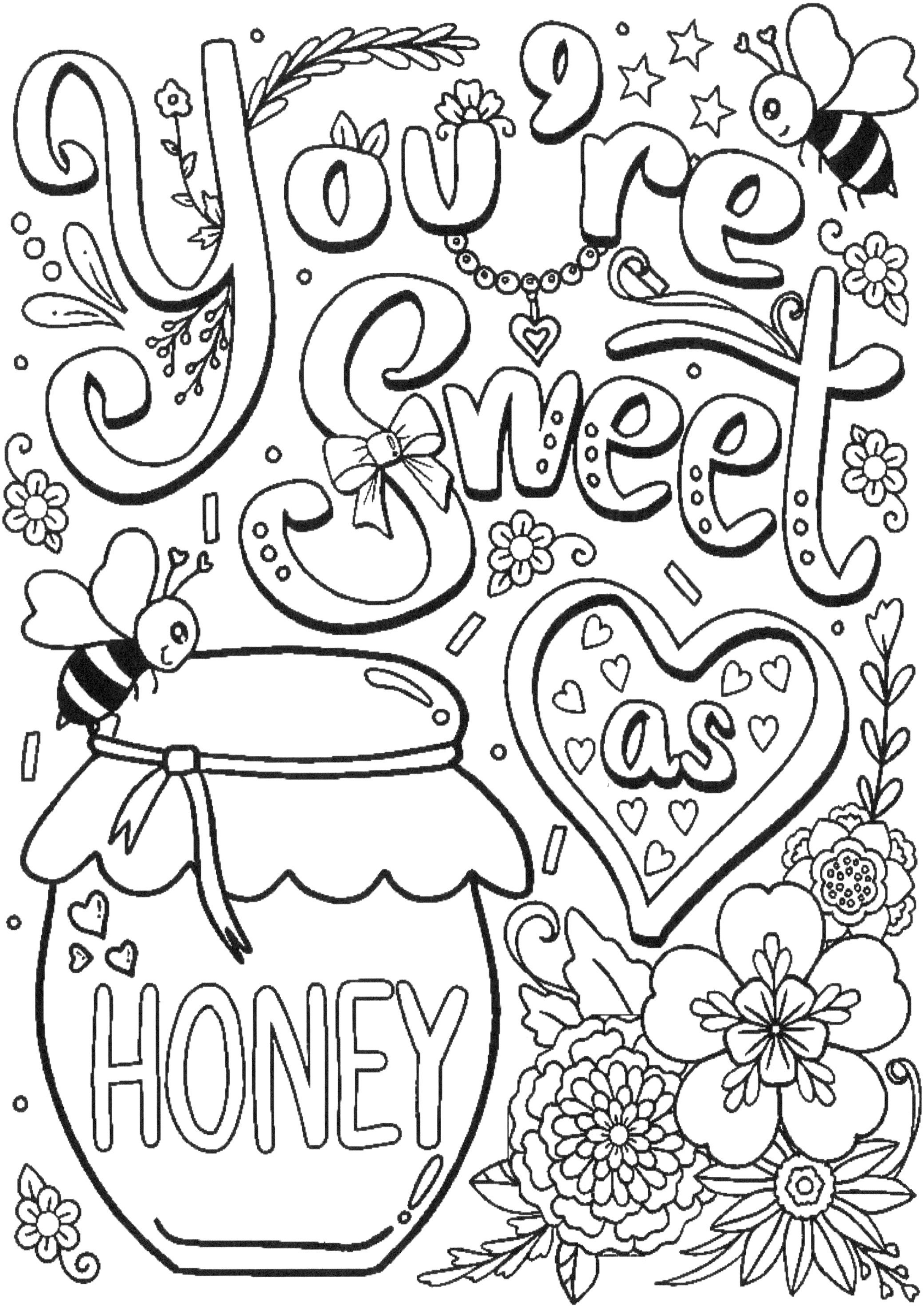
You're Sweet
as
HONEY

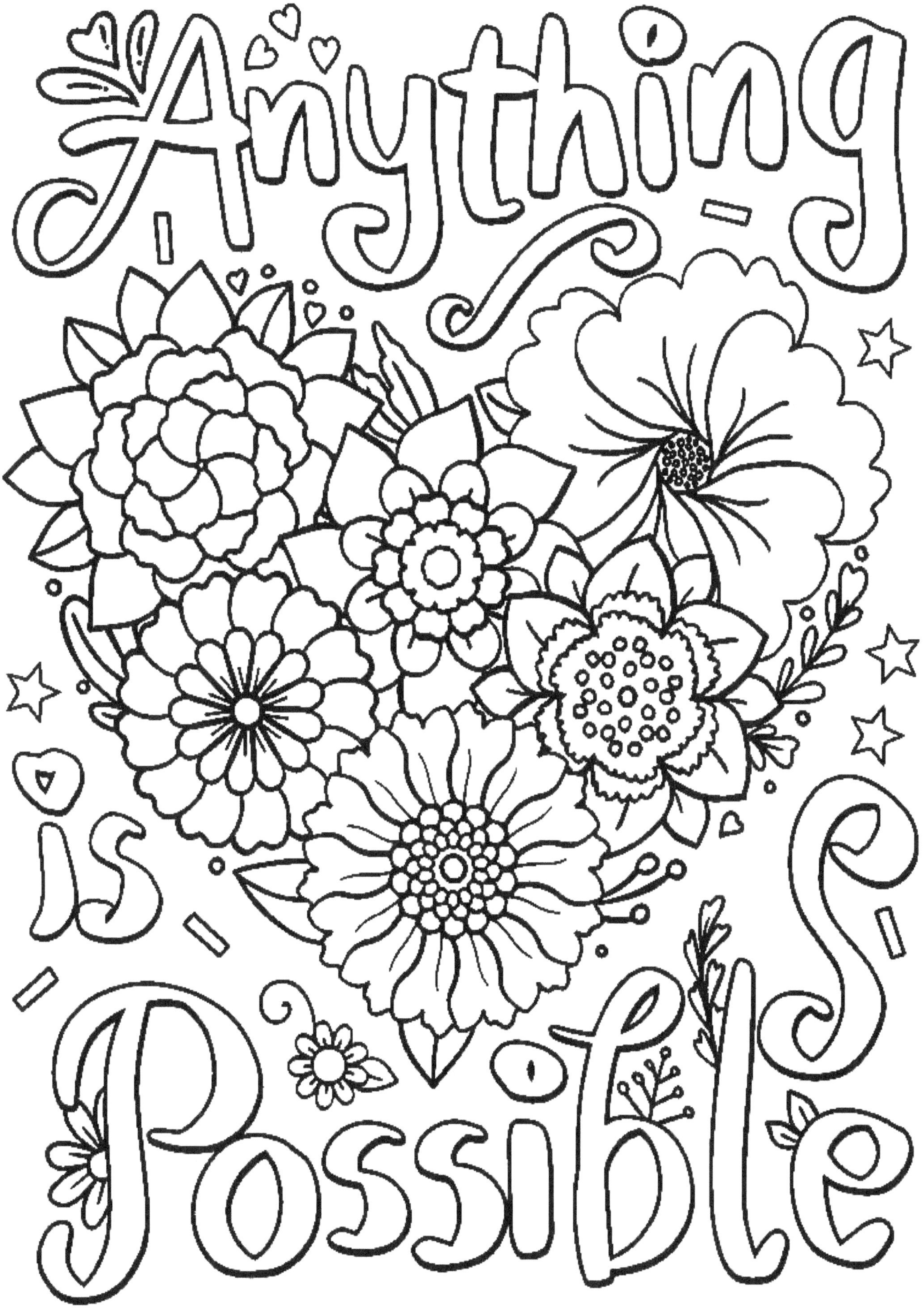
Anything
is
Possible

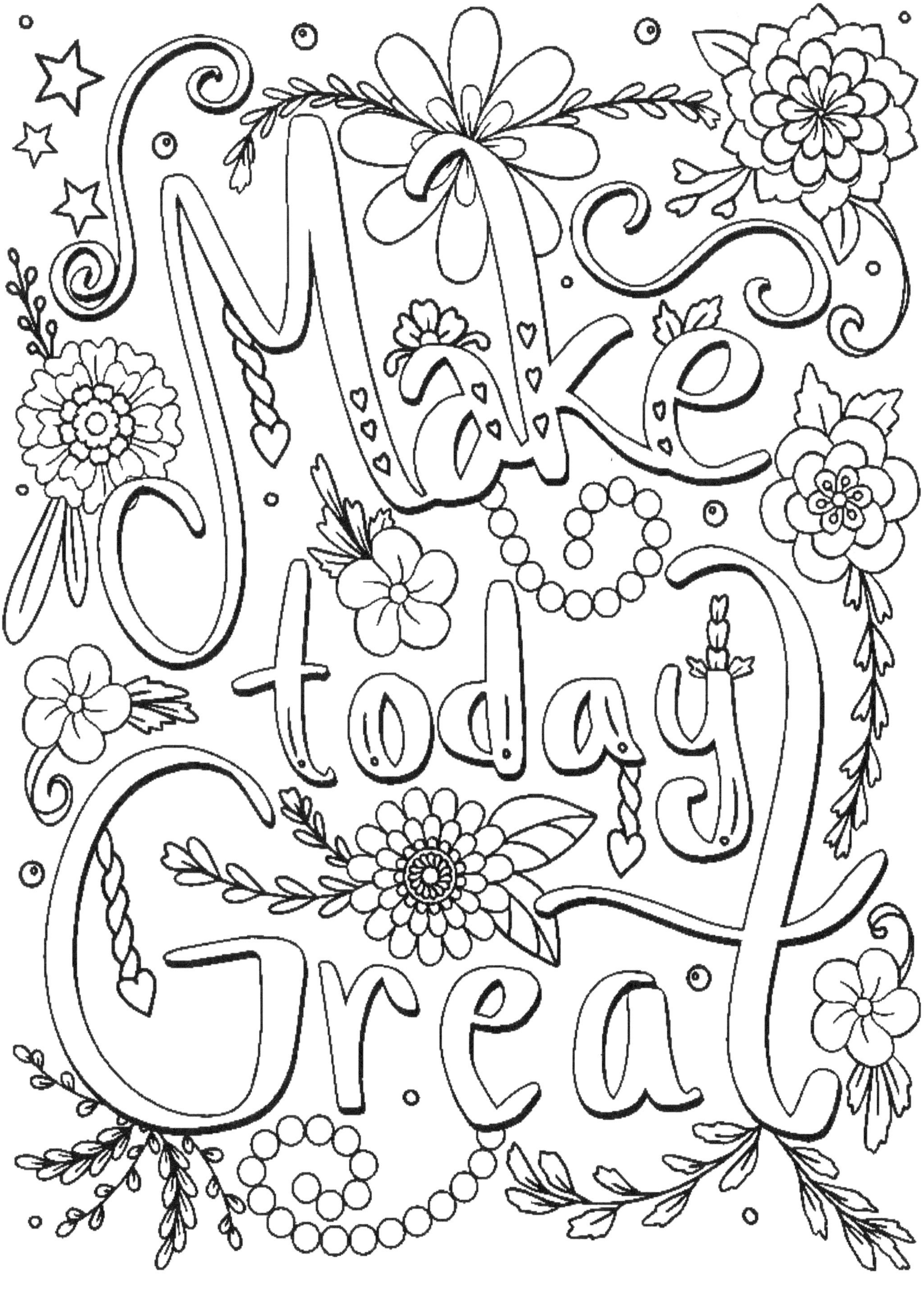
Make
today
Great

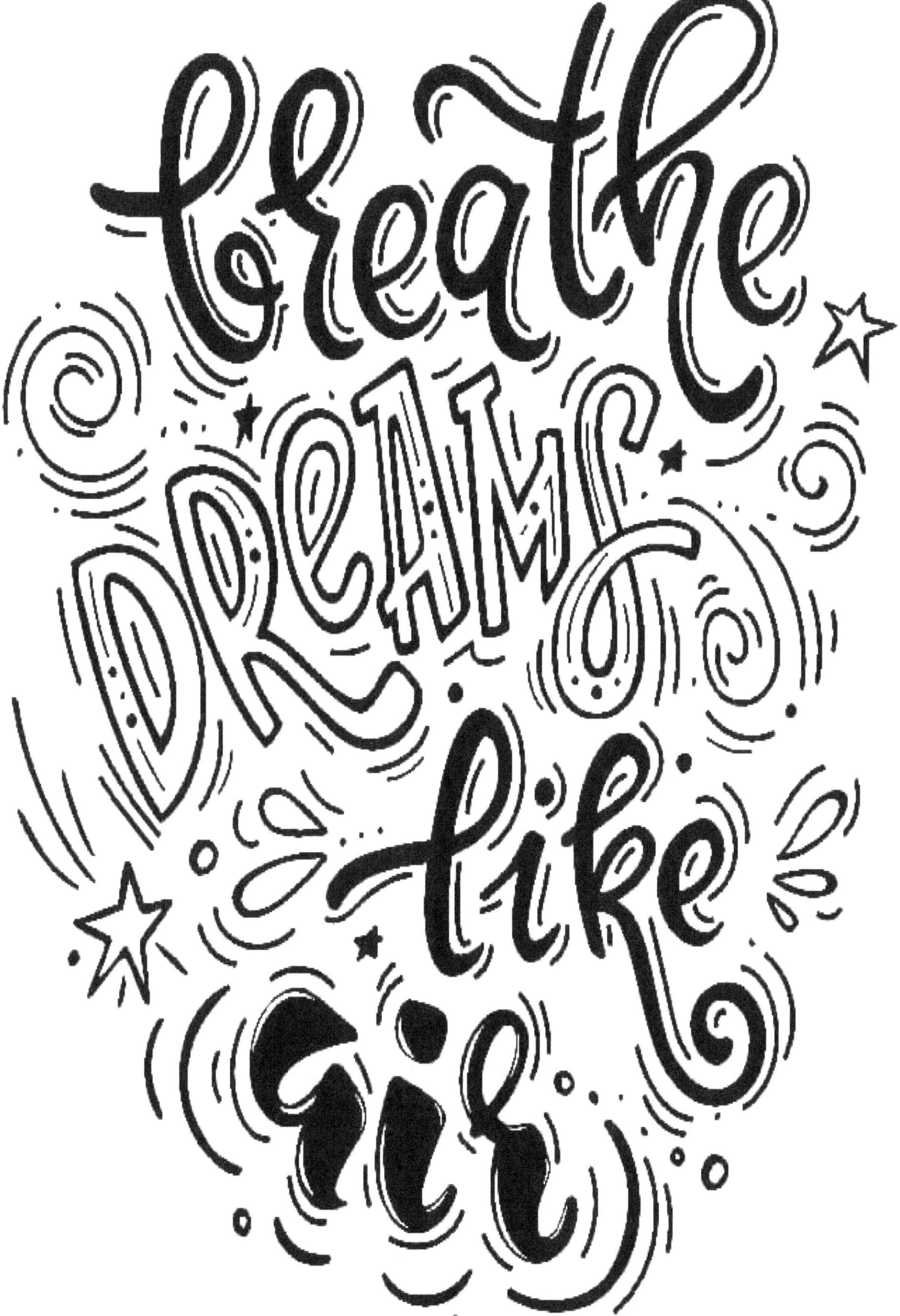
breathe
DREAMS
like
air

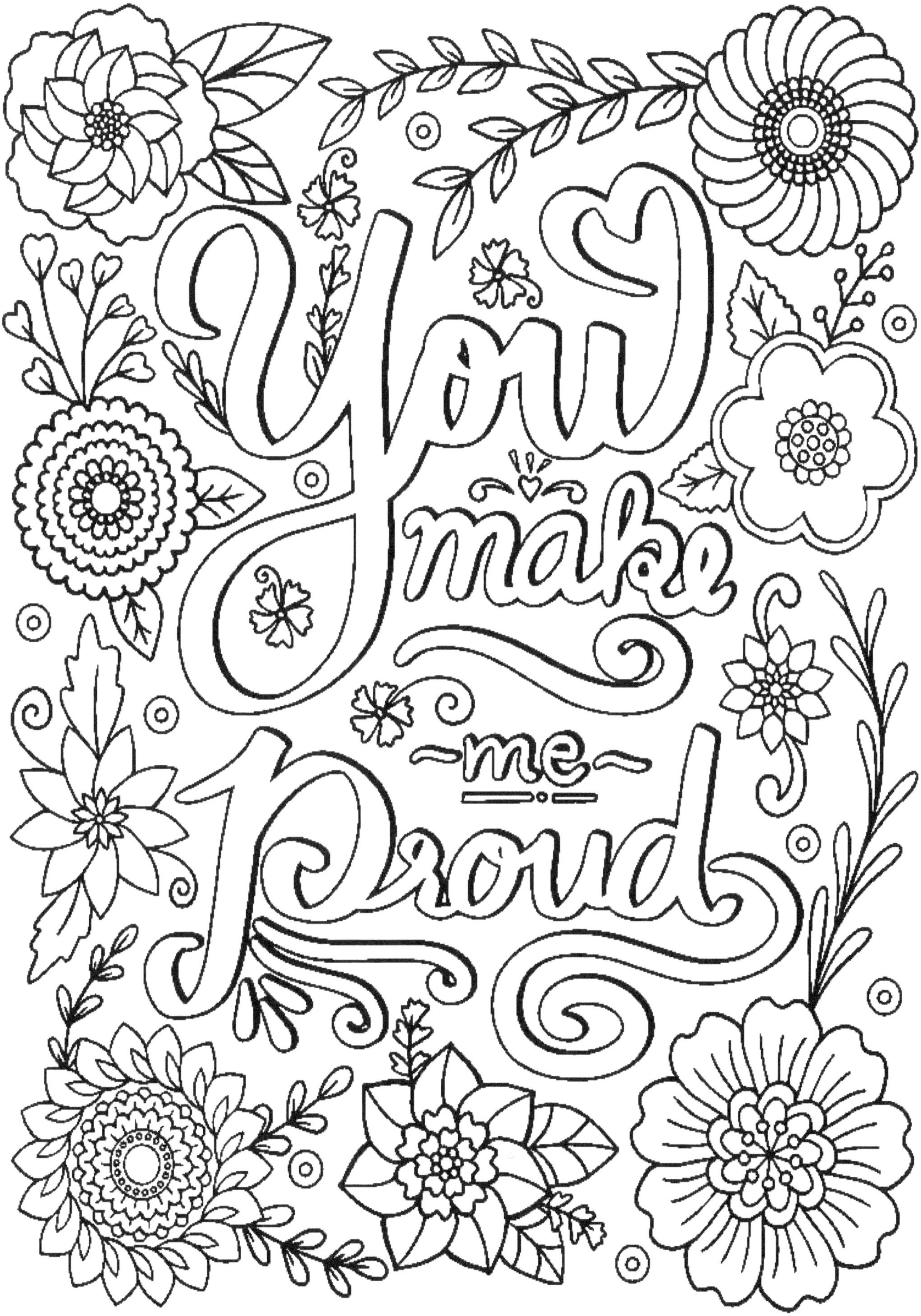
You
make
me
Proud

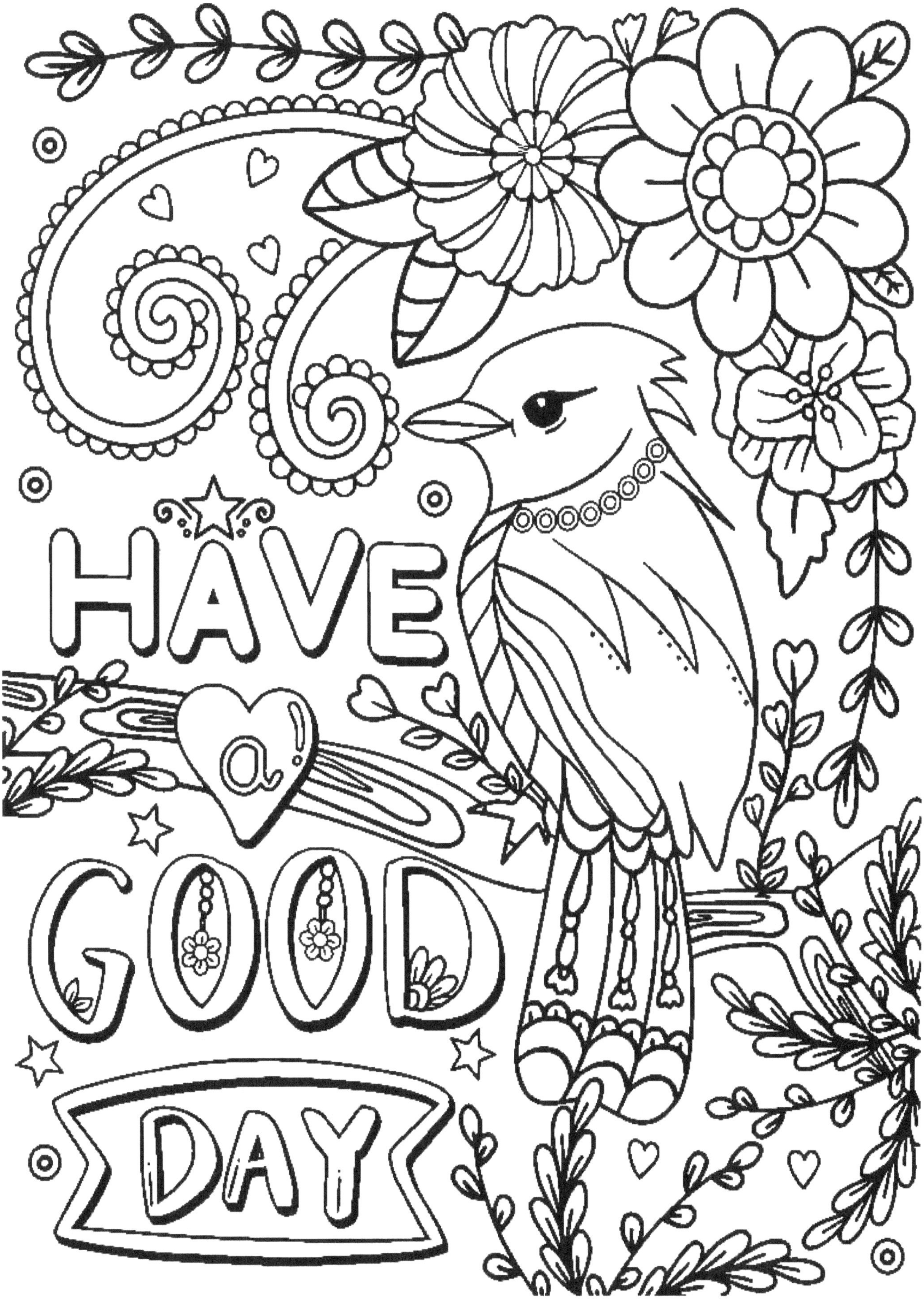
HAVE
a!
GOOD
DAY

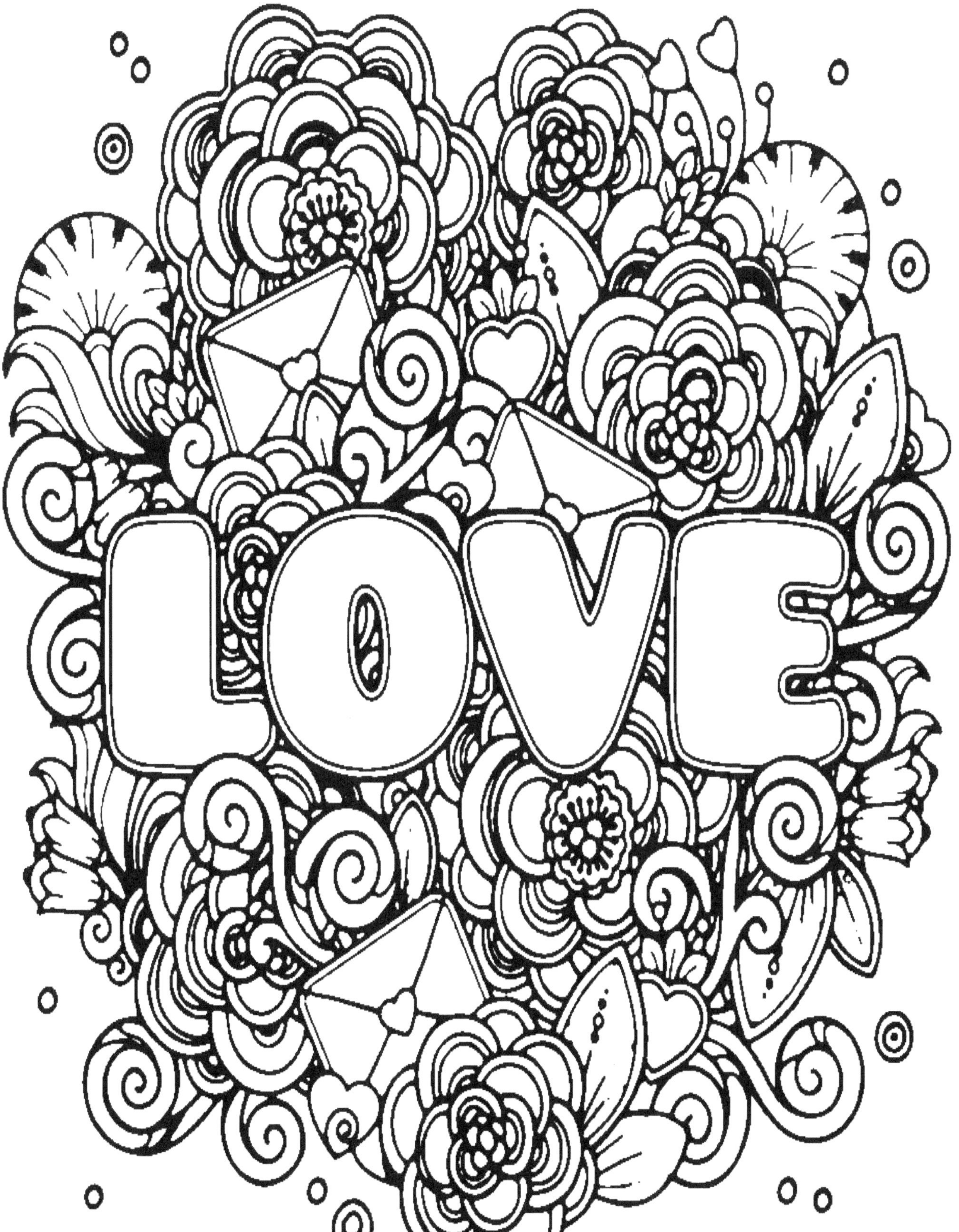
LOVE

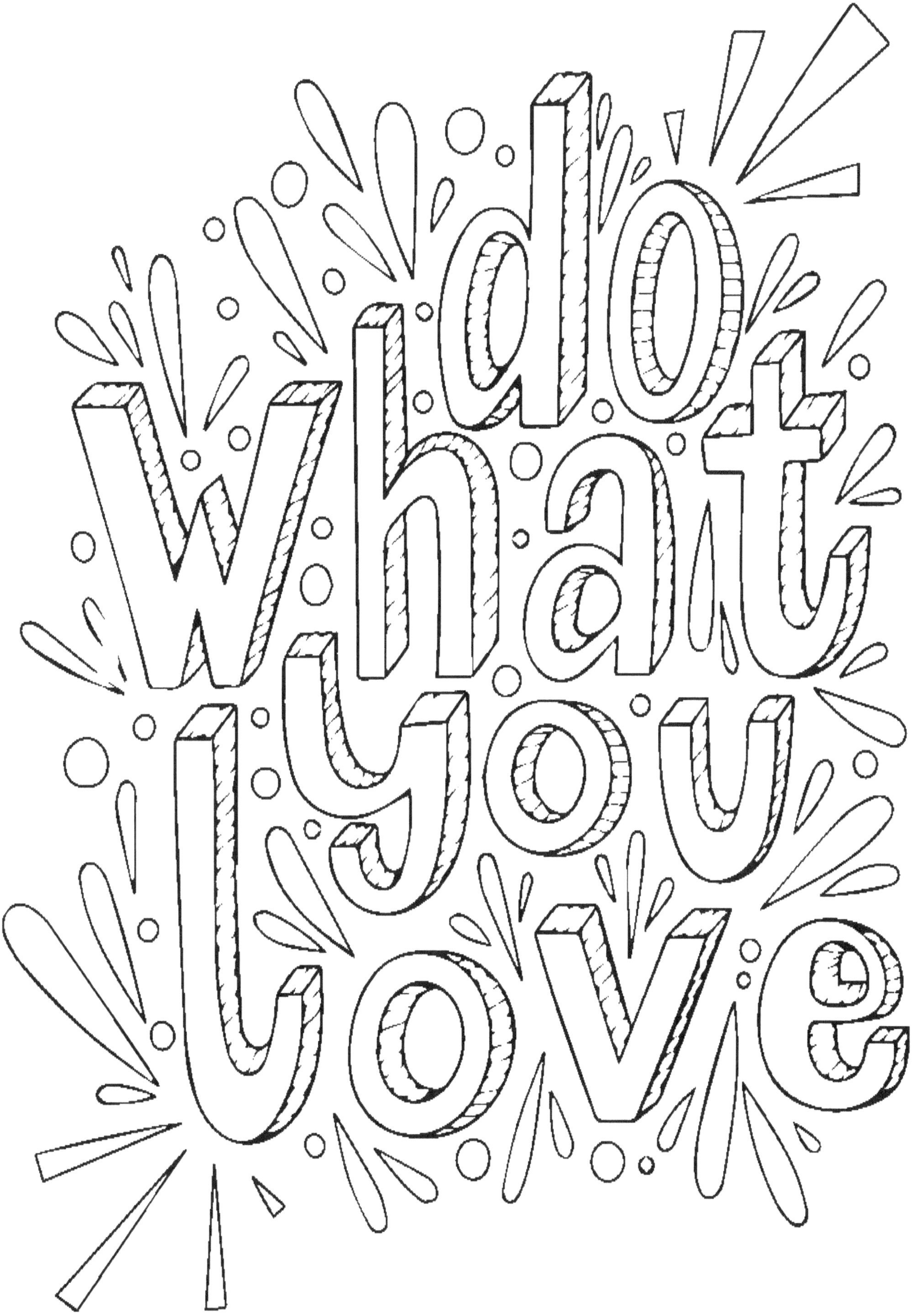
do
what
you
love

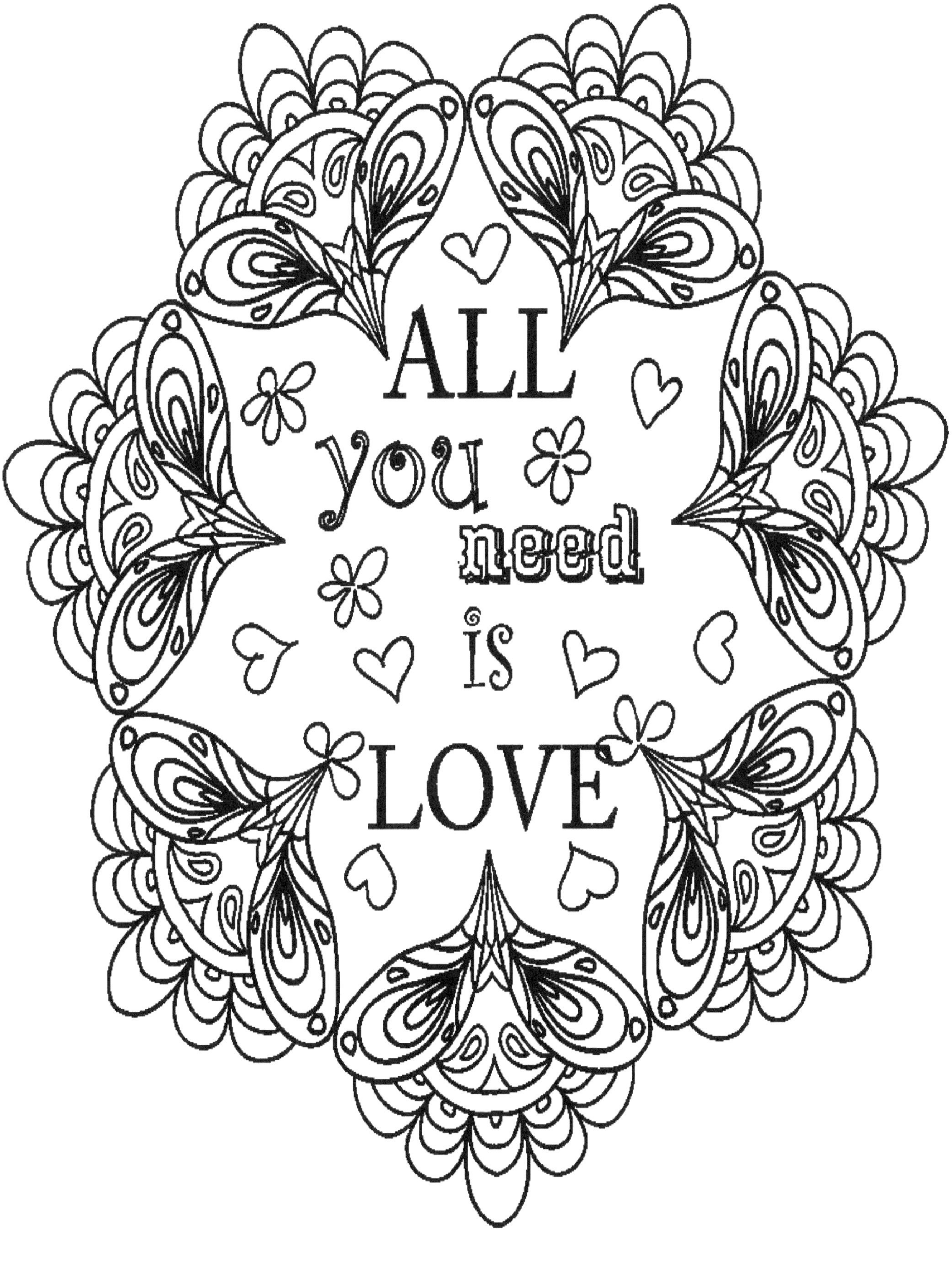
ALL
you
need
is
LOVE

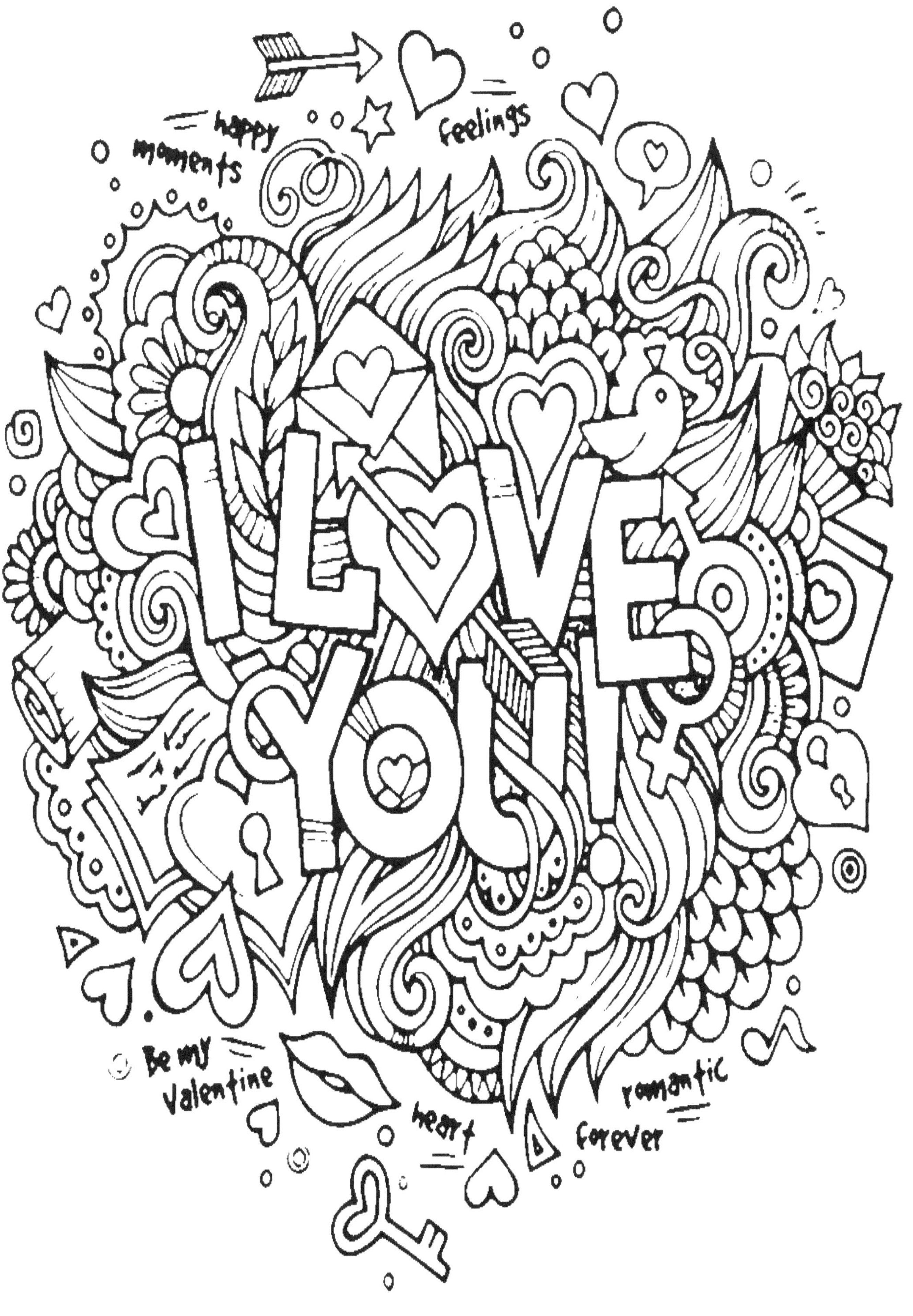
happy moments
feelings
I LOVE YOU!
Be my Valentine
heart
romantic
forever

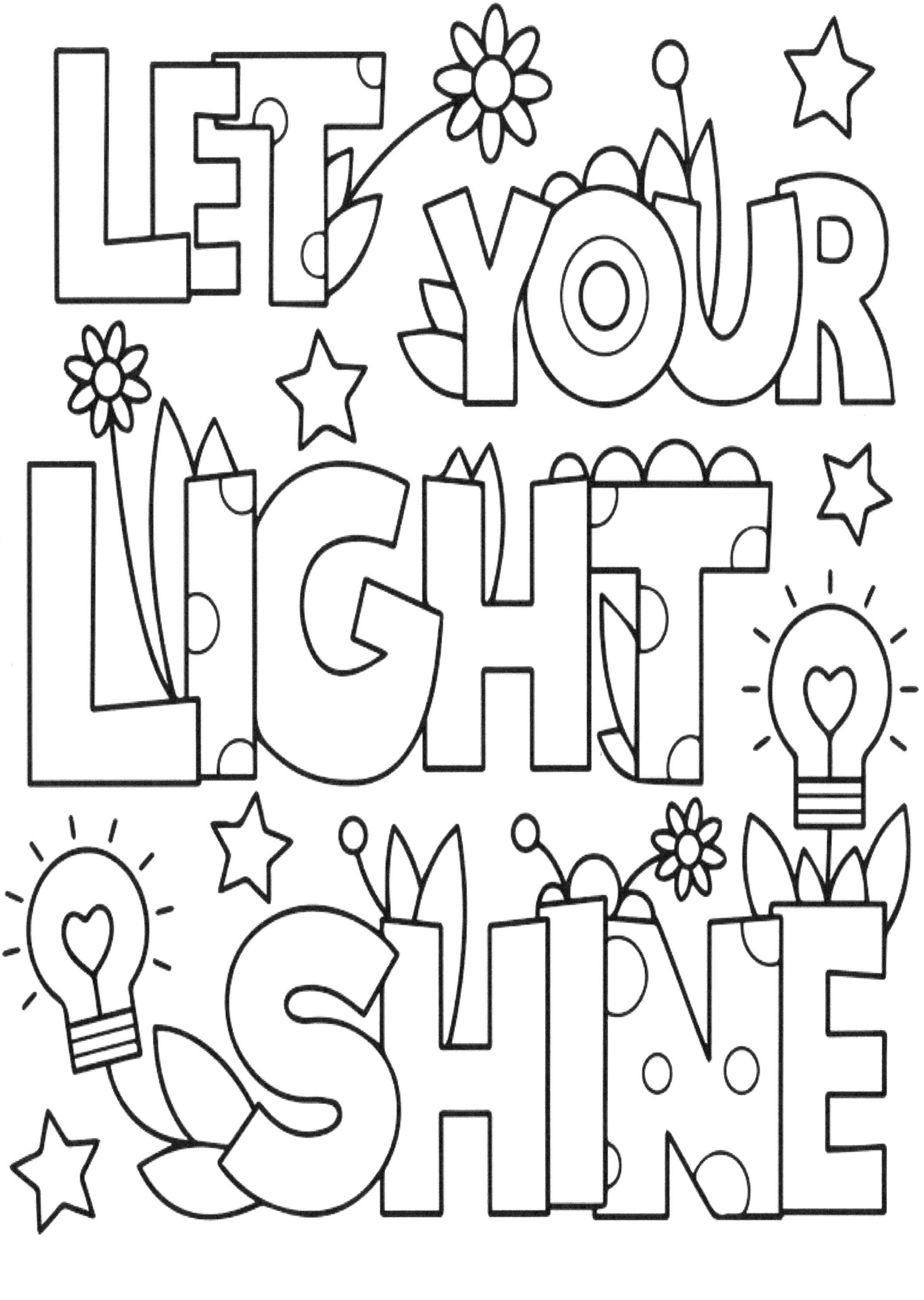
LET YOUR
LIGHT
SHINE

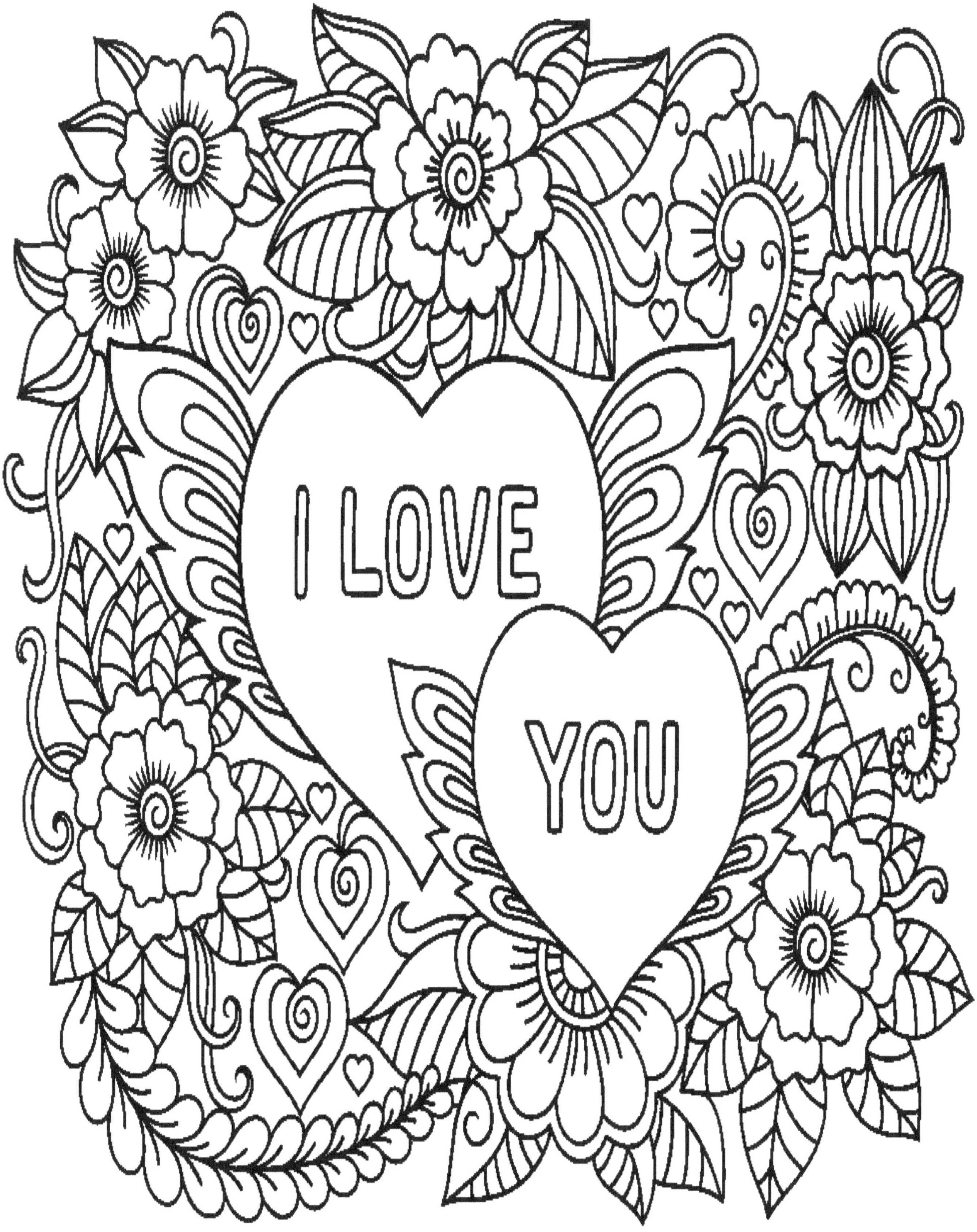
I LOVE
YOU

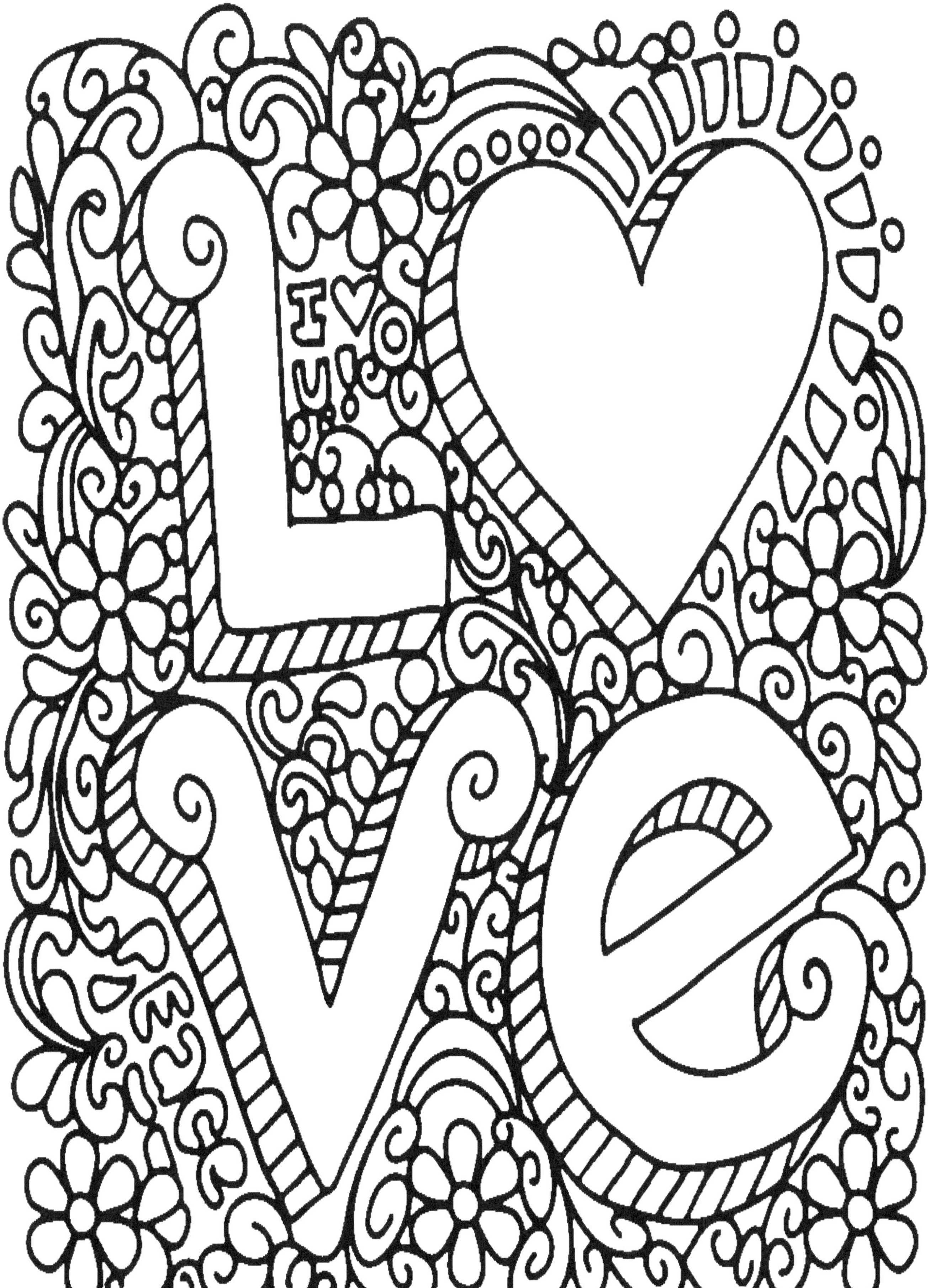
L♥ve

www.ingramcontent.com/pod-product-compliance
Lightning Source LLC
Chambersburg PA
CBHW081526220526
45467CB00010B/3070
9798712347186